THE BEST OF
OF
HAWAI'I'S BEST
SPOOKY
TALES

COLLECTED BY
RICK CARROLL

BESS
PRESS

3565 Harding Ave, Honolulu, Hawai'i 96816
(808) 734-7159 fax (808) 732-3627 www.besspress.com

Design: Carol Colbath
Moon logo from a design by Kevin Hand

Library of Congress Cataloging-in-Publication Data

Carroll, Rick
    The best of Hawaii's best spooky
tales / collected by Rick Carroll.
        p. cm.
    ISBN 1-57306-265-0
    ISBN 13 978-1-57306-265-7
    1. Ghost stories, American – Hawaii.
2. Tales – Hawaii. 3. Legends – Hawaii.
I. Title.
GR580.H3.C37 2006   398.25-dc21

Copyright © 2006 by Bess Press, Inc.

Printed in Korea

For John Sherwood, Felix Limtiaco, and Michael Dalke, the
lost members of Club Fugu

Contents

About Rick Carroll

An award-winning daily journalist for the *San Francisco Chronicle* and a frequent contributor to the *Los Angeles Times,* Rick Carroll has written West Coast headline stories on topics ranging from Haight-Ashbury's hippies to Silicon Valley's techno wizards. His dispatches from the Philippines during the Marcos era, published in the *Honolulu Advertiser,* won a National Headliner Award. His illustrated reports from Easter Island, Tahiti, and Huahine won honors from the Society of American Travel Writers and the Pacific Asia Travel Association.

Carroll is also the author of numerous Hawai'i and Pacific books on adventure, voyaging canoes, hula, island curiosities, and the supernatural. His collected "talk story" accounts of the supernatural introduced 150 local authors to print in the six-volume Hawai'i's Best Spooky Tales series. "The Passenger," one of Carroll's stories in this collection, appears in *Best Travel Writing 2005.*

After 20 years in Hawai'i, Carroll and his wife live in a nearly 300-year-old seaport village on an island with no name near Cape Lookout, North Carolina.

Introduction

Caution: The stories you are about to read may cause sudden chills, shortness of breath, increased heartbeat!

The Best of Hawai'i's Best Spooky Tales represents the epitome of Hawai'i's spooky tale genre and serves to introduce the whole collection to a new generation.

Here are 45 stories chosen from more than 200 stories in six best-selling volumes of *Hawai'i's Best Spooky Tales* and *Madame Pele: True Encounters With Hawai'i's Fire Goddess*.

Neither myth nor legend nor old "pork over the Pali" tales, these are true, first-person accounts of inexplicable encounters that happened—and are still happening—in Hawai'i today: stories that deliver a shiver up and down your spine. Or, your money back. That's the publisher's guarantee. Ten years and eight books later—no takers. Read on—only if you dare.

In "Old Hawaiian Graveyards," Nanette Napoleon meets a mystery man who takes her on a discovery tour—until she discovers he didn't! Keoni Farias describes a scary night he spent alone (or was he?) on a Maui beach in "Just Them Passing Through."

Doubtful folks who come face to face with Hawai'i spirits tell scary stories. Big Island author Gordon Morse reveals what happened to intrepid archaeologists exploring "Cliffside Burial Caves."

Travel writer Robert W. Bone shares a Bishop Street elevator with an invisible rider in "Giving the Ghost a Lift."

Don Chapman discovers new hazards when he tees off on O'ahu and Kaua'i in "Ghostly Golf."

Stories that startle true believers are especially chilling, like "A Moonless Night in Kona," by Madelyn Horner Fern, and Charles Kauluwehi Maxwell's *"Ka Hō'ailona."*

Woody Fern and Jeff Gere, two of Hawai'i's best-known

storytellers, relive uncertain days and nights in "Uncle Eddie" and "When Kona Winds Blow."

And Lānaʻi's favorite storyteller, Helen Fujie, offers her haunting memoir of "Roy and Pele." Gigi Valley takes you on a hike into Lānaʻi's spirit-haunted landscape in "Something Came between Them." You will also meet "The Halloween Waiter," who spooked me one night on Lānaʻi.

Kalina Chang recalls the day Israel Kamakawiwoʻole died in "Drums in the Night."

Hawaiʻi fire goddess, Pele, surprises Big Island visitors Julieta Cobb ("I Saw Madame Pele, in Person"), Barbara Swift ("The Lady in the Crimson Dress"), Michael Sunnafrank ("Pele's Gift to Liʻi"), and Dwynn L. Kamai ("Pele's Birth Announcement").

Some stories are too scary to read alone after dark. Simon Nasario describes "The Graveyard Shift at ʻEwa," one of three bone-chilling stories from Oʻahu plantation days.

Fox Lach presents characters that appeared in "The Dark Mirror" and Cheryl Z. Cilurso introduces "The Hitchhiker of Laupāhoehoe."

Eerie hula stories will make you squirm. A Maui hula troupe visits Laka's *heiau* on Kauaʻi and dances a hula it never knew in Akoni Akana's "Ghosts of Hula Past." A Lanikai *hālau* dances up a storm at the Merrie Monarch Festival in Lei-Ann Stender Durant's "Three Storms of Hina."

At Washington Place, the royal piano hits a sour note in "A Piano for Liliʻu," by Van Maunalei Love, whose son, Nicholas, wrote "My Grandfather's Ghosts" when he was 12.

Other stories are curious and poignant: "A *Pueo* Blessing," by Paula and Wayne Sterling, "A Hopi Elder Meets a Hawaiian *Kahuna*," by Charlene Peters, "Salt Box House," by Kaui Philpotts, and "Mystery on Maui," by Doug Self.

An old tale rings true when fireballs float across a Hilo bridge in *"Hitodama,"* by Gladys K. Nakahara.

A voice in the night tells a Kaua'i boy his father's dead in "Mamoru," by Richard S. Fukushima. And Carolyn Sugiyama Classen meets "The Spirit of Honokāne"; she also wrote "Disappeared."

Small-kid fears haunt George Y. Fujita in "Mu'umu'u," about a Maui fisherman with "no more hand."

Something happens to Nancy K. Davis and "The *Maile* Lei" when she takes a shortcut by 'Iolani Palace one afternoon.

On the night shift at a Big Island hotel built on sacred ground, Reggie Bello meets "The Elevator Man."

Visit the windward O'ahu neighborhood where Jerry and Debbie Kermode once lived with their son, Walker, at "Hale o Olomana."

Stop by "The Vacant Apartment" with Dennis Yanos to meet a chilly occupant.

Go to Pearl Harbor, where Thomas N. Colbath encounters "Arizona Ghosts." Then visit Moloka'i where Pam Soderberg discovers "Things Go Bump in the Night."

Finally, join me on the Kohala Coast and meet "The Passenger," a woman who knows too much about volcanoes; then spend "One Night in Pele's Garden of Woe," where the *kapu* on Pele's rocks is put to a test.

Not for the faint of heart, these ghastly epiphanies will prompt trembling and fear and cause sleepless nights. Those with *aloha* and *mana* will survive. Woe to the rest of you.

On Kaua'i's north shore on a knoll above the boulders of Kē'ē Beach stands a sacred altar of rocks, often draped with flower leis and ti leaf offerings. This altar, dedicated to Laka, the goddess of hula, may seem like a primal relic from the days of idols, but Ka Ulu o Laka Heiau is very much in use today. Often, dancers, men and women, of Hawai'i's *hula hālau* (schools) climb the cliff, bearing small gifts of flowers. Sometimes, a mother of a newborn will deposit the umbilical cord of her infant at this sacred shrine in a revival of the old Hawaiian ways, once banned by missionaries. In Hawaiian myths, Lohi'au, a handsome chief, danced here before the fire goddess Pele, and their passion became Hā'ena, which means "the heat." The site is filled with what Hawaiians call *mana,* or power. If you climb the cliff to visit this altar you will discover that you don't have to be Hawaiian to experience *mana.* But you must be *very* careful what you say and do.

Ghosts of Hula Past

This was at Kē'ē down near Hā'ena, the hula platform over there. I was invited. My cousin is a *kumu hula* on Kaua'i and they had their *hō'ike* for his *hālau* and there was a fund-raiser, a *hō'ike*, so he said come up. This was about eight, ten years ago. I had *keiki hālau* over here on Maui so he told me come up and do something, so we practiced over here real hard for that show, 'cause I was really excited about doing it. They was having it at Kaua'i Civic Center.

And when we went to Kaua'i I told the kids already that we was going to go visit the *hula pā* at Kē'ē before we go, you know, sometime before we do this show for them. So one morning we woke up early, no, we had a practice first. We had practice and, ho, they was just all off, and everybody was making me mad, was real, you know, I was yelling at them already, you guys, you did so well back on Maui, you come over here practicing, you so *moloā* all this kind. So we was feeling all junk but then I said, okay, we go out Kē'ē. So we all jumped in the van and went out there.

Had four mothers, five *keiki*, myself, and we went to Kē'ē and we hiked up to the top and then I did my *oli*, you know, the *mele kāhea*, the *mele komo*.

I went on top and I made them do their *mele kāhea* and I did my *mele komo* and I asked them to start dancing. So we had with us *kauna'oa lei* that I had brought 'cause Kaua'i no more *kauna'oa*, they have but little bit and hard to get. So I brought this *kauna'oa* and I made them put the *kauna'oa* on the back wall of this thing so they put their *kauna'oa* and I, we, had already decided what hula we were going to do and so we started chanting.

I started chanting this hula and all of a sudden I just like, I don't remember anything, I blacked out. I don't know what but I just—the chant was coming out but I certainly know, and even the mothers who was standing off to the side said, that wasn't you chanting. Somebody else was chanting.

Well, what happened was the kids danced this dance we never even know, never ever taught them, and the mothers was taking pictures, was like what's going on, so they was off on the side trying to take pictures of all of this and the kids when it was over, they all started crying. One started crying, the other started crying, they was crying they don't know what happened to them. They don't know what the chant that they did, so I explained to them that I felt that, you know, don't be afraid, was probably something good or something had come inside you and get you da kine, but I had all these crying kids.

The parents was all scared. They were like, kind of like being very defensive to me, like, you know, what you did to them? Or, what did you do wrong? Or, are we supposed to be up there? Or, what this and that? Nobody knew.

Anyway, on the way back we talked about it and I

was talking about it and I said it's a good thing, you guys should, like, don't think it's bad and this and that.

It's probably because it's meant to be and somebody, something came inside you and taught this hula and you learned something new even though you never remember exactly how it went but you just did it.

Well, anyway, what happened, too, that I didn't mention, when we left the *pā*, was coming down, when we turned to look at the mountain, da kine, the *kauna'oa lei* that we placed on top, were gone.

So, anyway, we talked about it on the way back and everybody got calm and good and that night we did the performance at the Kaua'i Civic Center and they were so good, they was like, was like wow! They brought the house down and everybody was like yelling 'cause they just were so good, they were perfect, no mistakes, they were so into it. It was a whole different group than what I brought over, it seemed to me.

Anyway, then we all came home and this and that and the mothers developed the pictures. And in the pictures that was the weirdest thing. Two different mothers took pictures, two different cameras. All the pictures were the same in the sense that all the faces, the kids and my face was white. Like white and the hair all standing up like this, straight up from the head in the picture and all you see is a faded thing up against the black cliffs of the *pali*.

So, all you could see was this white glow thing. So, when we saw that we all sat together and everybody cried 'cause was just like wow. So I don't know what it was, I don't understand it, I don't. I'm not *ma'a* to that kine stuff but I know that it truly, there was something that happened. And I know I will always remember that experience.

On the Big Island of
Hawai'i's Kohala Coast,
new resorts stand in lava
fields along ancient and
often sacred footpaths of
ali'i—as a young hotel
employee discovers when
he encounters . . .

The Elevator Man

In the summer of 1992, I was a housekeeper at one of the resorts along the Kohala Coast of the Big Island. I was only seventeen years old and had been working at the hotel for six months when this incident occurred.

Toward the end of the day, my manager asked me if I wanted to stay and work the night shift to help cover for a sick call. Even though I had never worked at night before, I agreed to stay and work a double shift. I was assigned to one of the towers in the hotel that night, and all I had to do was tend to the housekeepers.

The first two hours went smoothly. The sun had set, and now I was seeing the hotel in a way I'd never seen it before—darker, quieter, with different workers. I was on the service landing of the fourth floor, and I needed to go up to the seventh floor to pick up dirty linen from one of the housekeepers.

I pushed the "up" button on the elevator panel and waited for the one working elevator. There are two service elevators in the tower, but the one on the right (as you face the elevators) broke during the morning shift and had not been running all day.

To my surprise, the elevator on the right opened and out walked a tall, dark, Hawaiian-looking man, wearing nothing but a dark red *malo*. I didn't think much of it, since the hotel had so many workers in different uniforms. He acknowledged my presence with a simple nod. I walked into the elevator and pushed the seventh floor button. As the doors, closed I could see that Hawaiian guy still on the service landing looking at me.

The elevator went up to the seventh floor, but the doors did not open. Instead, the "SL" button lit up, and I started going down. (SL stands for "service level," which was the hotel's underground tunnel system.) It stopped at the service level, but again the doors did not open. Instead, the seventh floor button lit up again, and I was on my way back up.

The elevator kept going up and down without stopping. I started to panic. I pounded on the doors and yelled for help! I started to feel nauseous, because it felt like the elevator was going faster and faster. I then realized that the elevator had an emergency telephone located right under the button panel. When I picked up the telephone, it automatically dialed the Security Department. A security officer answered, and I told her that I was stuck in the elevator. She told me to hang on until an engineer got to the tower.

I stayed on the telephone with the officer until the elevator finally stopped on the fourth floor—where I had originally gotten on. I thanked the officer and hung up the phone. The doors opened, and to my amazement, that Hawaiian guy was still there! I walked out, and he started moving toward the elevator. I didn't even think about telling him that the elevator was acting weird. I was just so happy to be out. As he passed me, he let out a little laugh under his breath. He walked into the elevator, and the doors closed behind him.

I noticed that there was no sound coming from the elevator. It didn't sound like it was moving. Moments later, the other elevator opened (the one on the left), and out walked an engineer. He asked me if I was the person who was stuck in the elevator.

"Yes," I said, "but it was the other elevator."

He looked at me really weird and said, "What? That elevator was shut down all day for repairs. It's still not running!"

With his words, the image of the Hawaiian man and all the stories I'd ever heard about Hawai'i's haunted hotels ran through my mind. Did I just have a supernatural encounter?

You step into the elevator. Others enter, forcing you back, crowding you elbow to elbow with strangers. You stand quietly, staring at the back of the neck of the person in front of you. You wait for the elevator to go. That moment can seem like an eternity. Then the elevator door closes and up or down you go in silence, barely breathing until you arrive safely at your floor. Sometimes, though, the elevator stops at certain floors and nobody gets on or off. Is it only a mechanical glitch or are you . . . .

Giving the Ghost a Lift

Among the devices in the modern world that spook some folks are elevators.

It's not simply the claustrophobic effect of occupying a relatively confined space alone or with a group of strangers.

To those affected, to step into an elevator is to put themselves at the mercy of an unnatural environment in an unknown dimension—a sense of being placed in some sort of purgatory, where there is no ground, no sky, no sense of time of day, since neither daylight nor the darkness of the real world can be perceived.

"I mean, where ARE you really?" I was once asked by Mary Alice, a colleague at *Popular Photography* in New York, who had spent an unscheduled hour motionless between some floor and another in a nonfunctioning elevator.

Like many, I have been trapped in an elevator a few times in my life with little ill effect. Once, in Rio de Janeiro, I forgot that electricity was being rationed on a rotating basis in different parts of the city. When I went to visit a woman at her apartment one evening, I forgot to ask her what time the *falta* was scheduled to occur in her neighborhood. I simply had to sit on the floor in the dark and wait it out.

But to some people, elevators are more sinister.

Once in Puerto Rico, I was with several reporters traveling together in a single car over country roads long past midnight to check out a reported sighting of the Virgin Mary by some residents of a small village far into the interior of the island.

To keep ourselves entertained on this somewhat metaphysical trip, we told ghost stories. One particularly spooky one was related by Paul, whose aunt once had a terrifying experience. She was about to enter an elevator in a Chicago skyscraper when she noted with some alarm that the operator of the device was a skeleton.

Paul said his aunt was startled enough to decide to step back, whereupon the skeleton shrugged its clavicles and closed the door. The car suddenly plunged to the basement, killing all aboard.

Well, perhaps not all, I observed, since the skinny operator would seem to have been dead already. Paul was not amused, however. After all it was his close relative who had narrowly escaped death.

Another truism, subscribed to by many who occasionally turn their attention to the supernatural world, is that for some unknown reason, children are more sensitive to influences from beyond the grave.

Who hasn't heard of poltergeists who center their noisy and sometimes damaging habits on a child? Adults would never have seen the Jabberwocky, would they? Centuries ago, children so possessed were sometimes put to death by terrified populations.

One day in Honolulu these two volatile elements came together, the sensitive child, and the purgatorial elevator.

I think it was in that office structure at 1000 Bishop

Street where my son, David, then about ten, and I entered the elevator, perhaps on our way to visit Jeff Portnoy, an attorney who was handling a lawsuit I was bringing against my publisher.

David was equipped with a vivid imagination, and I held his hyperactive hand to make sure he did not dash off on the wrong floor. One or two of the small clutch of fellow travelers in the vertical dimension lowered their eyes from the set of numbers for a moment to smile at my handsome little boy.

Midway in our journey, the elevator stopped at a floor that had been chosen by none of us. The doors opened.

David stepped back. We all waited. The doors closed again, with no apparent change in the number of passengers. David spoke up in an even voice:

"Dad, a ghost got on there, you know."

If there was any conversation in the car, it ceased immediately.

"How did you know it was a ghost?" I asked, looking around at faces whose smiles had disappeared. All were listening intently.

"'Cause I could see right through him!" David replied.

There was a gasp or two of nervous, hollow laughter from those surrounding us.

One man quickly reached forward and pushed a new button for the very next floor. He apparently decided to leave immediately on an unscheduled stop. The rest of us decided to take our chances, and the door closed once more.

"Don't worry, Dad. It's all right," said David. "The ghost got off with him!"

When anyone asks what strange encounters I've experienced in Hawai'i I usually say, "Oh nothing really, stuff like that always happens to someone else." It's easier than admitting to uneasy moments on the "forbidden" island of Ni'ihau, or recalling the night a hand appeared in the zoom lens of my camera on a deserted Kaua'i beach, and the day I met a woman on Maui whose father missed his own funeral on Lāna'i. This story tells what happened the night I met . . .

The Halloween Waiter

I sat down to dinner one Halloween evening at The Lodge at Kō'ele, and the waiter appeared at my elbow. He looked so stiff and un-Hawaiian in his white dinner jacket, holding a burgundy leather menu.

"Good evening," he said—not aloha, but good evening in proper English.

"Hello," I replied, and smiled.

He handed me the menu and wine list.

"I can't tarry," I said. "I'm reading from my books after dinner."

"I know you are," the waiter said. "I've got a spooky story to tell you."

"I'd like to hear it."

"Certainly, sir."

It was the perfect place to be on Halloween, since The Lodge at Kō'ele was built on or very near an old graveyard.

The Halloween waiter began to tell me how when the Lodge first opened, an advertising agency hired a beautiful young woman and a handsome young fellow to pose as rich honeymooners.

"They stood outside their suite on the second floor and looked down into The Great Lobby," the waiter said. "They took lots of pictures.

"When the brochure came out, there was the young couple, but standing behind them were other people. Faint outlines of other people. Not shadows, other people. They threw away the brochures. Tossed 'em. Junk. Took new pictures."

"I'd like to see a copy of the original brochure," I told him.

"I have one at home," he said. "I'll bring it tomorrow."

Next day, the waiter called my room to say he'd looked everywhere and couldn't find the brochure, but that he would keep looking and he would call me when he found it. But I never heard from him again.

I told the young Filipino woman at the Concierge Desk the story I'd heard at dinner and she just hugged her arms, looked around to see who was listening, then said almost in a whisper. "There are many ghosts here."

I called Lāna'i the other day to ask the Halloween waiter if he ever did find that brochure but when I asked for him by name, I was told that nobody by that name ever worked at The Lodge.

Silversword, *nēnē*, and *'ua'u* are a few of the endangered species in Hawai'i. I warn visitors to the Big Island that incurring the curse of Madame Pele may put them on an endangered list, as well, in . . .

One Night in Pele's Garden of Woe

When the sun is at its zenith on the first Wednesday of each month, a time considered most auspicious in the Hawaiian calendar, a *kahu* on the Big Island of Hawai'i asks Madame Pele's permission to return yet another box of rocks to her Garden of Woe. That's what I call the newest landmark on the Kona Coast.

The garden, known locally as Ka Ahu Paepae o Hoaka Ho'omalu, is the final resting place for disturbed Hawaiian rocks. A disturbed Hawaiian rock, by definition, is one that has been taken from its original place in the Islands.

Every day boxes of disturbed rocks—*pōhaku* and *'ili'ili*—are returned to Hawai'i in the mail, always with a note of apology and a tale of woe.

For decades the rocks were sent to the home office of the Hawai'i Visitors Bureau in Waikīkī and forwarded to Hawai'i Volcanoes National Park rangers, who dutifully returned the rocks to Madame Pele's warm embrace.

Since all rocks in Hawai'i originate with Madame Pele, the fire goddess of the volcanoes, each rock is said to have *mana*, or supernatural power.

Some folks believe that if you take Madame Pele's

rocks something awful will happen to you. The belief is widely known as Madame Pele's Curse.

Now, everyone in Hawai'i knows that's *shibai*, a story created by a Hilo tour guide in the 1940s to frighten tourists, but you can't convince the folks who send the rocks back. They believe the rocks caused them grief.

And so the rocks keep rolling in across the Pacific to end up here on a swale of black lava on the grounds of the Marriott Outrigger Waikoloa Beach Resort between the ancient fishponds of 'Anaeho'omalu and the Waikoloa petroglyph preserve.

The site of the rock repository was chosen because of its unusual geographic position in the archipelago. It sits at the *piko*, or navel, of the surrounding volcanic peaks of Haleakalā, Mauna Kea, Mauna Loa, Kohala, and Hualālai.

Only the peak of Kīlauea Volcano, where Madame Pele's been dancing on the East Rift Zone since 1983, is out of sight, although her smoky breath darkens the sky on Kona days when the air is still.

●●●

To this almost sacred place, for the last three years it has been my good fortune to be invited on Halloween to tell true, first-person tales from my six spooky books.

Usually, I tell spooky stories in gathering darkness under rustling palm trees on the black lava seacoast. This time Noelani Whittington, in an obvious attempt to test my nerve, asked the hotel staff to set up lawn chairs next to the new rock garden.

I decided to take a look at this new venue and found a pile of red and black volcanic rocks, some smooth as

glass, others porous as a sponge. Each rock represent-
ed trouble for some sorry wretch.

I tried to guess which rock caused a Douglas fir tree
to crush a Puyallup bungalow, a head-on Porsche crash
in La Mesa, a slip-and-fall in a Kennebunkport bathtub,
and the premature death of a Primadonna cocktail wait-
ress in Reno.

All the rocks looked innocent, the sort of stones
anyone might pick up and take home as a souvenir of
Hawai'i. The power of these rocks, it appeared, had been
spent.

After sunset—in what passes for a dark and stormy
night in Hawai'i—nearly one hundred souls huddled
together under flickering tiki torches while a hard wind
swept down from Mauna Kea's summit.

I pointed out the rock garden and told how rocks are
considered special in Hawai'i, how they have spiritual
power, and that the rocks they saw here had all been
returned to Hawai'i by unfortunate souls who claim
they fell victim to Pele's Curse.

Everyone looked at the rocks. Some gave a little
shudder. Tell you more about the rocks later, I said.

I then told true stories about night marchers who
follow trails on the Kona Coast, of pressing spirits who
hold you captive in your bed, of old bones and stones
and things that go bump in the night.

Soon everyone was holding their elbows, shivering
in the tropic night, experiencing that delightful spine-
tingling sensation folks in Hawai'i call chicken skin.

I told Nanette Napoleon's "Old Hawaiian
Graveyards," Dr. Phil Helfrich's *"Limu Make O Hāna,"*
and Dominic Kealoha Aki's "The Night Madame Pele
Visited Hanauma Bay."

I told how the wrong body ended up in a casket at a Lāna'i funeral and how the skeleton of an old fisherman caused migraine headaches in Waimea.

Everyone wanted to hear more Pele stories. One man wanted to know "the real story" about Pele's rocks.

"First, you need to know the truth: the story of Pele's Curse is a fiction, invented by a Hawai'i tour guide here on the Big Island. The story has no basis in fact in Hawai'i legend. That is true.

"And this is true: bad things often happen to people who take Pele's rocks. Some people lose their jobs or their homes, have terrible accidents, end up in the hospital, die. The rocks you see here were returned by those unlucky folks.

"So, now, we have two opposing truths, and in the end, it is up to you to decide what to believe.

"I've got a great idea," I said. "To prove Madame Pele's Curse, true or false, let's get up, go over to the rocks, pick one up, and take it home.

"Keep it for a year, until next Halloween, then let me know what, if anything, happened to you. Okay, let's all go get a rock."

Everyone laughed nervously. Nobody moved.

"What's the matter?" I asked.

"I just told you Madame Pele's Curse isn't true. Nothing will happen to you. C'mon, let's all get a rock."

Nobody moved.

"I don't believe this," I said, grinning. "All of you believe in a story made up by a tour guide?"

Everybody giggled. Nobody moved.

"Okay, here's an easier way to test the veracity of Madame Pele's Curse. Let's all go get a rock and take it to our room. Keep it overnight. Put it back in the morning. Just let me know how you slept. Okay?"

Nobody moved.

"What's the matter?" I asked. "You don't believe me?"

A hand shot up from the back row.

"You shoulda been a lawyer," a fellow said.

Everyone had a good laugh.

Nobody took a rock home that night.

The road to storytelling can
sometimes be as spooky as
the stories themselves.
Hold on tight as I pull
over to pick up . . .

The Passenger

She stood in shimmering heat waves along Queen Ka'ahumanu Highway on a hot October day. I couldn't believe anybody would be standing in the sun at high noon on what seemed like the hottest day of the year. I thought at first the woman in the white dress might be a mirage. Dark skin, the color of coffee, Caribbean maybe; black hair in dreadlocks, she looked real as a rainbow. She stuck out her thumb and I stopped.

●●●

My day full of strange encounters began in Honolulu at the airport. A security guard wanted to inspect my carry-on.

"Oh, I love your books," she said, finding only spooky books in my bag. I gave her one. She gave me a *mahalo*, and waved me through.

On line at Starbucks a Charles Manson look-alike, one of the terminal's homeless denizens, hit me up for three dollars. He wanted "a wet, double tall, French vanilla latte." His outrageous request made me laugh. I gave him a buck.

While waiting for my coffee I was paged repeatedly:

" . . . please return to the security gate." I finally got my coffee and went back to find I'd dropped my ticket to Kona during the security check.

I ran to the gate only to find my plane was late. By the time I got to the Big Island the Budget rental car outfit was out of cars.

"We have a ten-passenger van you can have for the same price as an economy sedan."

"It's just me," I said.

"It's all we have," the clerk said. She handed me the keys to what looked like a Roberts Overnighter tour bus.

●●●

That's how I came to be all alone driving an air-conditioned van big enough for ten people on Queen Ka'ahumanu Highway on the Big Island of Hawai'i on a hot October day.

My destination was Waimea School, where I'd been invited to read from my books as part of the Marriott Outrigger Waikoloa's annual spooky "talk story" event.

I saw the hitchhiker just after leaving the airport. With an empty ten-passenger van, I decided to give her a lift.

I stopped, she got in, and I immediately felt something was wrong but didn't know what. The chilled van seemed warmer with her aboard.

"Where're you going?"

"Waimea," she said.

"Me too," I said.

"Do you live there?"

"No," she said, "just visiting."

She was neither young nor old, but somewhere in between, with caramel skin, charcoal hair, bright, clear eyes and a soft voice that sounded like music.

She carried neither suitcase nor backpack, only a white canvas bag stuffed with newspapers and magazines, and handwritten notes on yellow legal pads.

She had a musty aroma of sweat and something flammable. I thought the rental van had a gas leak.

•••

Queen Kaʻahumanu Highway is unique in Hawaiʻi. The two-lane black asphalt not only runs through twenty miles of black lava landscape, but also crosses over several layers of historic lava flows and under four of the island's five volcanoes—Kohala, Huālalai, Mauna Loa, and Mauna Kea. Pele land if there ever was.

Most passersby see only a bleak charcoal expanse, but my passenger knew and identified each and every lava flow with evident pride as if each flow were an object of art in her private collection.

"Kaʻūpūlehu flowed to the sea in 1801," she said as we passed under Huālalai Volcano. "It filled Kīholo Bay . . ."

" . . . and the 1859 Mauna Loa flow ran from nine thousand feet near the summit to the sea . . . "

" . . . the Kanikū flow covered Waikoloa and ran into the fishponds at ʻAnaehoʻomalu . . . "

Although I had no way to verify the truth of her words, her keen recitation startled me.

"How do you know all this?" I asked.

"Just do," she said. "It's my hobby."

We rode in silence for a mile or so. I half expected

her to ask for a cigarette—a common request from Pele, the fire goddess.

"Don't you want to ask me for a cigarette?'

"I don't smoke," she said, smiling.

We rode on in silence.

"Are you sure you're not Madame Pele?" I finally asked. I couldn't help it.

"Oh no," she said. "I'm not Madame Pele."

"How do I know?"

"Believe me," she laughed.

"I'm not sure I do," I said.

In misty rain, we approached Waimea town. She said good-bye and thanks at the T-intersection.

"I'll get out here," she said at the stoplight. She opened the door and jumped out. She cut across the corner gas station; I half expected the gas pumps to burst into flames.

That never happened. Something just as startling did. As I watched her walk away, she disappeared. Vanished into thin air. One minute she was there, the next she was gone, like that. I asked the gas station attendant if he'd seen the woman in white.

"No, brah, see nothing."

I found Waimea School library full of kids waiting to hear spooky tales that Friday afternoon. The library was cool and quiet, I was hot and sweaty.

"Are you okay?" one of the librarians asked. "You look like you've seen a ghost."

"I'm not really sure, but I think I just gave a ride to a woman who may have been Madame Pele."

The librarian had a sympathetic smile. "I know," she said. "It happens a lot here."

That night at a dinner party hosted by Patti Cook,

who knows everybody in Waimea, I told my story to the other guests and asked if they had ever seen the woman hitchhiking along the Queen's highway or walking in their town.

Now, Waimea's a very small town, and surely someone would have seen a woman in a white dress with dreadlocks who knew a lot about old volcanoes, but nobody ever had, at least that's what they told me.

The day Iz died the people of Hawai'i were grief-stricken. Some said a prayer, others wept. One woman, home alone after dark, heard the unmistakable sound of . . .

Drums in the Night

It started out as a morning like any other. I got up around six or so and turned on the radio. It then became a morning like no other. The news reporter said, "We are sorry to report the death of singer Israel Kamakawiwoʻole . . . ." My eyes filled with tears as I stood there, not wanting to believe what I heard. How could our "Hawaiian Sup'pa Man" suddenly be gone? Anyone who listened to Hawaiian music was aware of his health problems, but somehow we just weren't expecting him to die, not now, so young.

People, most of them choked up, began calling in to Hawaiian 105. Other stations were getting calls as well. KINE put through a call to the Mākaha Sons, who were in Las Vegas at the time. Their shock and sadness reflected the reactions here as they grieved for the loss of their friend and former band member. Throughout the day, Iz's music was played across the Islands.

The following evening I was home alone, my husband at work on swing shift. We are in the last house on the road, next to the jungle at the foot of the Koʻolau Mountains. The windows and sliding door are nearly always open. It was after seven, and dark at the time. It was quiet in the house, as I had turned off the radio.

I thought I might watch TV, and picked up the newspaper listings.

That's when I heard the drums. They sounded clear and very close, like right outside. There were two sets of the same beats. I went out on the upstairs *lānai* and listened. I turned on the outside light. I saw nothing and heard nothing more. There is nothing out there but dense jungle. My backyard is not accessible from the road.

The next day Iz's music was still being played on the radio in heavy rotation, and I heard the song "E Ala Ē" (the original version).

I suddenly realized that the drumbeats in the beginning of the song were identical to the ones I heard the night before. There was no one home but me at the time, so no one else to testify to it. I hesitate to tell people—they usually think I was dreaming—but I assure you I was plenty awake.

So I wonder: Was this his way of reassuring me (and anyone in earshot) that he was still with us? I have heard others say that they still feel his presence, and I believe that this will always be so.

Eh, Iz, how we miss you.

When Arnie Palmer and Jack Nicklaus built championship golf courses in Hawai'i, they had no idea Hawaiian ghosts would be a major handicap or that chicken skin is par for the course. And if an elderly Hawaiian gentleman starts talking to you on Kaua'i's Po'ipū Course, heed his words.

Ghostly Golf

There have been times that I'd have sworn my golf swing was haunted by an ancient Irishman named Mulligan, but until recently I'd never put golf and ghost in the same thought.

Then things started to, well, happen.

And all of a sudden, certain things started making sense.

Like the time that Craig Stadler made a four-putt bogey after driving the green of the par-4 13th hole of the Kapalua Bay Course during the Lincoln-Mercury Kapalua International. Stadler, one of the stars of the Professional Golfers Association Tour and a former Masters champion, smacked his tee shot 300 yards to within 40 feet of the pin. Thinking eagle and no worse than birdie, Stadler putted short, then long, then long, and at last barely lipped in the fourth putt.

This kind of stuff just doesn't happen to PGA stars. So for years I chalked it up to Just One of Those Weird Deals That Happen Sometimes.

But then not long ago I was back at Kapalua, researching a story on the Maui resort's certification as an Audubon Society Cooperative Sanctuary, and started talking with a couple of Bay Course greenskeepers, Kimo Kiakona and Arnile Libunao. As they tell it:

It was still dark that morning as they put out pins and tee markers on the 13th and 14th holes.

"I seen 'em first, this white thing," said Arnile. "At first I thought a water pipe had busted, or maybe the sprinklers were on. It looked like water shooting up, except there was no sound."

He immediately called Kiakona, a native Hawaiian.

"I saw this white thing, like walking toward me, taking steps. But when I turned the headlights of the cart on it, there was nothing there," Kiakona said. What was it? Nobody knows.

Now Hawaiian culture is rich with ghost stories, and Kiakona said his elders have talked about seeing ghosts and that this one fit their description.

"I know it was one ghost," he said.

In the pro shop, they weren't sure if it was Casper the Friendly Ghost or if they should call Ghostbusters.

At about the same time, on the other side of the West Maui Mountains at Sandalwood, a Hawaiian warrior clad in loincloth and gourd helmet was suddenly appearing to golfers, materializing at the edge of trees lining the seventh hole à la Shoeless Joe Jackson in *Field of Dreams*. While the story has been widely repeated on Maui, neither professional Fran Cipro nor anyone on his staff has ever seen the apparition.

"I heard one story about eight guys seeing this thing and leaving in such a hurry they forgot their clubs and carts out on the course," says Cipro. "That's just never happened."

If you believe that spirits linger about graveyards, then there certainly is a chance that ghosts get into golf. The 13th hole of the Klipper Course at the Kāneʻohe Marine base runs between the sea and a sandy hill that is an ancient burial ground for Hawaiian royalty. The second and sixth holes of Oʻahu's municipal Kahuku course skirt an old cemetery. The third and fourth holes at the Bay Course run past a large, grassy mound that is believed to be home to the largest burial ground in the Hawaiian Islands. The dune that runs between the sea and the 17th and 18th holes at Poʻipū Bay, Kauaʻi, is home to old bones. The course also includes two *heiau*, or ancient temples.

And then there are the "birthstones" located in a thicket of dense jungle above the 15th hole at Koʻolau Golf Course at the windward base of the Koʻolau Mountains. The stones are actually boulders, large enough to fill a room, carved in the exact likeness of the towering mountains above.

Five hundred years ago and more, Hawaiian women went there to give birth, and as they awaited their time they carved the stones. I took a Hawaiian *kahuna* friend, Kawena Young of Hilo, there, and as she walked among the stones running her hands a few inches from the surface of the stones, the hair on the back of her arms stood straight up.

"There is heavy *mana* here," she said. Then, holding her hands above one rock in particular, she said: "There's so much *mana*, here, it tingles, it almost hurts."

Later, she chanted and thanked the spirits for allowing us to be there and asked for their blessing. Now Koʻolau is officially the toughest course in the United States and probably in the world, so there's no other reason than Kawena's chant to explain why I have always played that hole well and with luck.

Twice, I've had severely sliced tee shots bounce out of the jungle on the right of the hole and onto the fairway. Another time, an approach shot struck way too strong, hit a tree at the back of the green, and dropped into the grass, from where I chipped in for birdie. Heavy *mana*, indeed.

But that's not the heaviest *mana* story that I've heard about on a golf course. That distinction goes to a series of stories told to me while I was covering the PGA Grand Slam at Po'ipū Bay for *Golf Week* magazine. Greg Norman, Nick Price, Ernie Els and Jose-Marie Olazabal were about to tee off on the second day of the 36-hole competition. I waited beside the first green when an older Hawaiian gentleman walked up and started chatting. He wore the arm band and carried the "Quiet Please" paddle of official course marshals. He said that he had helped build the Po'ipū course as well as several others around the islands as a bulldozer operator.

"Every time I have to break the *'āina* (the land) I always tell the spirits 'I'm sorry, but this is how I make my living,'" he said.

Sometimes, the spirits listen, sometimes they don't.

"On this course, three times, we had funny things happen, things you can't explain. "There's two *heiau* on the back nine, one on the shore by 16 and 17, the other inland by 10. Three times, on pretty flat ground, we had Caterpillars tip over. There's no way to explain it but it happened."

He continued:

"I spent three years in the hospital after one accident on Lānaʻi. Lots of funny things happened there, too. One time I was working on the course there and there was a sacred site. My Cat flipped over on me. I almost died. Years went by, I wasn't healing, so finally I called a *kahuna* and she came and I got better."

He added that friends of his had worked on the H-3 Freeway on Oʻahu.

"They kept moving a big rock and when they come back the next day, it's there again. That rock wanted to be there. They finally hauled it away. The guy who had it moved was from the mainland. The next day, he was walking where the rock had been and a small branch fell out of a tree overhead and fell down and poked out his eye."

By this time the PGA Grand Slam foursome was approaching the first green, and I had to get to work. I thanked the gentleman for his stories and asked his name.

"Only if you don't use it," he said. I promised and he gave me his name and his son's phone number where he could be reached.

When Rick Carroll asked me to contribute to this book, I wanted to confirm some details of the old gentleman's story, so I phoned the son on Kauaʻi. He was flabbergasted.

"When did you talk with my dad?"

"November of 1994," I told him.

"That's impossible," he whispered. "He died in 1993."

You never know who or what you may encounter when you stop to give a hitchhiker a ride on the Big Island of Hawai'i, especially if the hour is late and the road to Hilo town is dark, and you are the only soul on the highway. Cheryl Cilurso takes us for a chilling ride in this unusual spooky tale about . . .

The Hitchhiker of Laupāhoehoe

On a crisp and clear morning, shortly past the midnight hour, a young man in his twenties travels alone along the dark stretch of the road leading to Hilo town on the Big Island of Hawai'i. As he passes Laupāhoehoe he sees a figure in the distance that appears to be hitchhiking along the side of the deserted highway.

Upon nearing the figure he realizes that it is a woman dressed entirely in black. She wears a long hooded coat and long black gloves. Feeling she is in distress, he pulls over and offers her a ride. She graciously accepts.

The dark of the early morning sky doesn't enable the young man to get a close look at her, but trusting that she is harmless, he continues along. After having traveled awhile in complete silence, the driver tries in vain to make conversation with his passenger.

Deciding she has probably fallen asleep, curiosity overwhelms him and he wants to catch a glimpse of the quiet stranger. Not wanting to take his eyes off the road for too long, he cautiously leans forward and is unprepared for what he finds: nothing but darkness peering out from behind her hooded cloak.

Beginning to worry and unsure of what is taking

place, he glances down at the rest of her and realizes she doesn't have any feet.

Panic-stricken, he yanks the vehicle over and rushes off to find a pay phone. Upon returning to the car, he finds she has disappeared.

Feeling vulnerable and frightened, he decides it would be better to drive the rest of the way home than to stay in the middle of nowhere, alone, until the morning comes. In shock, he gets back into his car and forces himself to continue. Inside the car he finds himself shivering and rolls up the windows to keep warm. Funny, he thinks to himself, that he hadn't noticed how cold it was outside. But the inside of the car continues to get colder even with the windows rolled up.

Unable to keep his mind off of the ghostly passenger, he glances down to where she once sat. In her place remains an indentation, as if someone is still sitting next to him.

While her colleagues press on into the uninhabited valleys of the Big Island's Kohala Coast, a weary backpacker remains behind in Honokāne Valley enjoying the solitude—until she hears the faint strumming of a guitar and looks around to discover no one there, only . . .

The Spirit of Honokāne

I was born and raised in North Kohala on the Big Island of Hawai'i, and as a child spent many hours playing on the black sand beach of Pololū Valley. This is a remote, wet valley (previously used to grow taro and rice) on the windward side of North Kohala, where the road ends at a scenic overlook. No one has lived in this valley and the other valleys to the east for years.

During the summer of 1973, I was an archaeology student at the University of Hawai'i at Mānoa, doing research in Pololū Valley on a National Science Foundation stipend. The other researchers and I also backpacked into Honokāne Nui, the next valley over, and Honokāne Iki, the smaller valley east of Honokāne Nui. So I was familiar with these uninhabited valleys and their trails. I lived in Pololū for three months that summer and continued to hike into the valley thereafter.

Several years later I decided to hike with three other friends into the valley. We hiked into Pololū, then over into Honokāne Nui. I do not recollect meeting anyone on the trail into the second valley. The others wanted to see Honokāne Iki, but since I was tired, I chose to stay by myself on the pebbly beach of Honokāne Nui.

I was sunning myself on the deserted beach when suddenly I heard loud guitar strumming. I sat up and looked around and shouted, "Who's there?" There was no answer. I was startled because I did not see anyone on the beach near me, but the guitar strumming continued.

I looked up into the sky. There was no plane or helicopter or anything near me. Then the strumming stopped. I did not see anyone else on that beach.

When my three friends returned about half an hour later, I did not tell them of the incident, as I was afraid they would scoff at me. Incidentally, none of us had a guitar with us.

We then hiked up the ridge between Honokāne Nui and Pololū and then way into the back of Pololū to a secret swimming hole I knew of. While we were eating lunch and swimming at this pool, which is way off the main trail, one of my *haole* friends turned to me and said, "I hear a guitar strumming."

I stared at him and felt chicken skin go down my back. I couldn't hear the guitar he was talking about and neither could the other two people. Then I told them about what had occurred on the beach of Honokāne Nui, now miles away.

Frightened by this mysterious guitar strumming, we quickly packed up our knapsacks and hiked out of Pololū. We didn't hear any guitar strumming after that, and did not see anyone on the trail out of Pololū Valley, but we felt that a spirit had been following us on the trails.

In Hawai'i people often hold picnics in graveyards; they bring food and drink and spread a blanket to spend the afternoon with dear, departed family members. Sometimes, like this devoted daughter, they bring their deceased relative a favorite food. She always brought her father's favorite dessert to his grave in a Big Island Buddhist cemetery. And each time it . . .

Disappeared

My beloved father, Dr. Francis Sueo Sugiyama, passed away on May 8, 1996. Dad was born in a small plantation village called Hala'ula in North Kohala on the Big Island. He grew up there, graduated from Kohala High School, attended the University of Hawai'i at Mānoa, and later got his dental degree from the University of Maryland. Because he loved Kohala, he returned to practice dentistry and orthodontics in Hāwī for thirty years.

We all remember his favorite dessert—sliced bananas topped with peanut butter. Dad would eat this several times a day. He belonged to the Kohala Jodo Mission in Kapa'au, where his parents, two brothers, and sister-in-law are at rest in the cemetery. So, of course, when he died, he was buried in this same small graveyard, next to its charming Buddhist mission in rural Kapa'au.

Something mysterious started occurring during the summer of 1998. Because Dad used to loved bananas so much, Mom began leaving a whole, unwrapped banana at his gravesite. One day Mom left a banana, as usual, on a small "table" on Dad's grave, which usually holds incense and other offerings in keeping with the

Buddhist religion. Four hours later I stopped by to put flowers on Dad's grave, but nowhere did I see a banana. When I asked my Mom where she had put the banana, she insisted that she had left it as before, on the little table.

A few days later, my thirteen-year-old son, Stephan, and I left another banana at Dad's grave in the morning. When Mom visited in the early afternoon, the banana had once again disappeared.

Later that month, Stephan hid a banana under a fern that was growing on Dad's grave. This was a fairly large fern, and you couldn't see the banana when you walked by the grave. The next morning we anxiously returned, to find no trace of the banana. I felt chicken skin going down my back at that moment. Perhaps it was Dad's ghost eating the banana, and not a human thief as I had suspected, since a thief never would have seen that hidden banana.

This disappearance of the banana from Dad's gravesite went on all summer. Was it Dad's ghost returning from the dead to enjoy his favorite dessert? Japanese-Americans believe in *obake*—spirits—and maybe this was a spirit that loved bananas. Nothing else was ever taken from the grave, even though we left other fruit. Nothing else was ever stolen or disturbed on his grave. No banana peels or other evidence of an eaten banana was ever found next to his grave or in the vicinity of his grave. And this is not a graveyard on a major road or one visited by many people. Members of that Buddhist mission are rarely seen there during the day or evening, and, anyway, no member would dare steal from a grave. Usually we are the only ones at the cemetery when we go to place flowers on the graves.

We have never been able to discover what or who was taking those bananas. Perhaps it was a graveyard *obake* after all.

Living among believers and skeptics are the rare few still caught unawares by the legends of Hawai'i. Julieta Cobb was one of the few until after her first visit to Volcanoes National Park, when she could say with certainty . . .

I Saw Madame Pele, in Person

When I came to the United States in the spring of 1991 from the Philippines, I knew nothing about Hawai'i lore. I had never heard of Madame Pele.

In early 1992 my husband, Dwight, and I went to the Big Island for a visit and to do some sightseeing. We spent the night in Hilo, and early in the morning we drove up to Volcanoes National Park. It was still early when we got there, so we decided to go to Volcano House hotel and restaurant for breakfast.

We were the first ones to eat, and when we finished eating I told my husband that I wanted to use the restroom. I went down a hallway from the dining room to the restroom. I entered the restroom and proceeded to a stall.

When I finished, I opened the door to the stall and saw a tall woman with long black hair and a long white dress standing by the sink. I had not heard her come in.

She did not speak to me, so I did not speak to her. I washed my hands and left. She was there the entire time, but didn't move—to go to a stall or wash her hands or anything. She just stood there without moving.

When I left the restroom, I saw my husband standing in the main hallway. I went to him and asked if he had seen a tall Hawaiian woman go into the restroom. He told me nobody had gone into the restroom; she would have had to pass him to get there.

Just then I turned and saw a large picture on the wall. It was a picture of the lady I had seen in the restroom.

"There she is right there," I told my husband. "Is she the owner of this hotel or something?"

He told me, "That's Madame Pele, the Hawaiian goddess of the volcano, not a real person."

When I told him I had just seen that lady in the restroom, he told me that was impossible. He was laughing at me, and I was getting angry with him because I knew what I had seen.

About that time a Korean lady who was opening the gift shop overheard us talking. She came over and asked me what I had seen. I told her that I had seen the tall woman in the picture in the restroom, but that my husband wouldn't believe me.

She did not laugh at me. She told me this had happened before with people who are attuned to it.

Since this incident, I have read a lot about Madame Pele. But I don't care what I read or what people say. On that morning in that hotel restroom I saw Madame Pele in person.

On a postcard-perfect day in Hawai'i, an Air Force veteran visiting his daughter on O'ahu makes a pilgrimage to Honolulu's most famous war memorial, the USS *Arizona*. While reading names carved in stone, he is startled to hear voices of young sailors, voices that can only belong to . . .

Arizona Ghosts

As we left Camp Bellows bound for Pearl Harbor to visit the USS *Arizona* Memorial, it was another of those beautiful days in Hawai'i that attract people from all over the world. My wife, Shirley, and I were in Hawai'i to visit our daughter, who lives on O'ahu. We were filling up the days that she had to be at work by taking in the usual tourist sites.

The trip across the island from the windward side via the Pali Highway was beautiful, the traffic wasn't bad, and we found the parking lot for the memorial without any problems.

The boat ride across the harbor was pleasant, and the view of the memorial as we approached it was impressive. I thought the concept of an open-air structure spanning the sunken ship was a magnificent idea that brought one close to the tragic events of that day.

I was not at all prepared to be so deeply moved as I was by the chapel-like room at the end of the memorial where the names of those who lost their lives on the Arizona were carved into the stone wall. As I was reading some of the names, I began to sense the presence of two sailors between me and the space between the guardrail and the wall where the names are inscribed. I couldn't really see anything, but I knew the sailors were there, and I could almost see their uniforms. I felt the hair on the back of my neck standing on end, and I wondered if anyone else felt their presence or if I was having some sort of hallucination. I tried to focus my eyes on them, but there wasn't anything of substance to focus on; however, I could hear their voices. In a pleading tone they were asking, "What happened? Where are we?"

A moment later they were joined by a third sailor, who I felt was trying to communicate directly with me. I still get goose bumps (what people in Hawai'i call chicken skin) when I remember the intensity of the imploring look in his eyes and his melancholy plea, "I want to go home. Please help me go home." I had the sensation that they didn't realize they were dead, and couldn't figure out what had become of them. They were asking for help. I wanted to reach out to them, to let them know they had been dead for over fifty years and were free to move on—but how?

This encounter brought tears to my eyes, and it was all I could do to keep from sobbing out loud. My feelings obviously showed, because Shirley asked me if I was upset because I had known someone on the *Arizona*. I didn't when we arrived at the memorial, but now there are three who will be very close to me for the rest of my life, even if I never learn their names.

H urrying across the grounds of 'Iolani Palace at high noon, a Honolulu woman experiences an inexplicable incident with . . .

The Maile *Lei*

My first job in Honolulu was as a lei maker at the airport. When I started work there, I was told *maile* should never be entwined with anything else.

Some years later I worked at Queen's Medical Center. Just before lunch hour I was told a co-worker was having a birthday. I ran downtown to buy a lei for the occasion. The lei maker entwined *maile* and *'ilima* leis that I had selected.

I noticed the clock and was worried about getting back to work in time. So I grabbed the leis and decided to take a shortcut through 'Iolani Palace.

A few steps onto the 'Iolani Palace grounds I felt a cold, forceful hand on my right shoulder. When I turned around fast, I got chicken skin and dropped the lei.

Then I realized no one was even near enough to grab me. But when I reached down to pick up the leis, the two leis were separated in the plastic lei bag that had been sealed with a tie and ribbon at the lei stand.

Ever since that incident, I have observed deep respect when at 'Iolani Palace and have practiced good lei etiquette.

For one whole year dancers of Hālau Mohala 'Ilima practiced "The Three Storms of Hina" in preparation for the Merrie Mōnarch Hula Festival. They learned every nuance of the *hula kahiko* and chant, perhaps too well. As they danced in competition on a rainy night in Hilo, the sky broke with lightning and thunder and the lights went out. Shaken, the hula dancers gave up their chance to win rather than risk the wrath of . . .

The Three Storms of Hina

Are you superstitious? Do you believe some things just cannot be explained? Do you believe in the gods and goddesses that are a part of Hawai'i's folklore?

I never considered myself to be a superstitious person. If I searched hard enough, certainly I would find an explanation for everything. I grew up listening to the legends my *kupuna* told. The gods and goddesses in these stories belonged to a time that was behind me and these legends were a record of all thing's past. Things from my ancestors' past would never belong to the present, so I gave little thought to any of it—not until one night in April 1986.

I was one of 24 dancers of Hālau Mohala 'Ilima and we were in Hilo for the Merrie Monarch Hula Festival. We were a close-knit group, and after nine months of training together, we were ready to share our hula with the crowd gathered at the Edith Kanaka'ole Stadium. Our *kumu*, Māpuana de Silva, and her husband, Kīhei, had prepared us well, and we were excited to be participating in the "Olympics" of hula.

The *hula kahiko* competition number, which eighteen *wahine* groups were going to present, was "Pu'inokolu'a Hina" (The Three Storms of Hina). The chant speaks of Hina, the goddess who guards the island of Moloka'i.

Hina keeps the sacred wind gourd, "Wawahonua," and when the people mistreat the land, she opens the gourd slightly to release its first storm. "Trees are uprooted and thrown over . . . shrubbery is twirled, sweeping down and out to sea." Hina waits for the people to improve, but they don't. Hina opens the gourd cover halfway to release the second, stronger storm, "causing skies to darken . . . lightning flashes, thunder cracks . . . wild gushes of wind causing ocean floods." There is little change in the hearts of the people, so Hina opens the gourd cover all the way and "the worse storm is released; crushed are the chief, crushed is the land." (Of the three winds associated with the storms —'Ilinahu, Uluhewa, and Luluku—only the last one, Luluku, is a destroyer of man. This final destruction is how Hina protects her beloved land of Moloka'i).[1]

The weather in Hilo during the Festival of 1986 was unlike the weather of previous years. Yes, Hilo has a lot of rain, but this time it was different. As I recall, during the Miss Aloha Hula competition on Thursday night, there was a soft breeze blowing through the stadium and the rain was nothing but a light mist. Nothing seemed unusual. The Hilo rains continued all day Friday, and by Friday night the rain was coming down a little harder, the wind was picking up, and things were looking a little ominous.

As we dressed and prepared for our performance, we could hear the other *hālau* take their turn on stage. With every performance, the weather seemed to

---

[1] Description taken from Kīhei de Silva, "Hula Kahiko—Pu'inokolu'a Hina," *Merrie Monarch Fact Sheet.*

worsen. I wondered if there was a connection between what was happening on stage and the weather conditions. Were the dancers merely telling a story or were they becoming the storm? The chanting and dancing continued, and the storm intensified. The pelting rain was now accompanied by strong gusty winds, spectacular shows of bright lightning, and deafening sounds of thunder. I began to feel uncomfortable.

I sat alone and thought about this chant and remembered the difficulty I had in mastering the dance, difficulty I had never experienced with any of the other chants I learned over the years. I didn't enjoy this chant or this dance because I was having such a hard time. During our performance we would be taking the role of storytellers and focusing on the love Hina has for the land. We would not, in our dance, become those three storms. The dance we learned was to be done with calmness, but I never felt calm.

My thoughts were interrupted when the lights went out just before the intermission. We were dressed and ready to perform, but there would now be an indefinite delay. I remember a strange silence at first and then the emcees were doing their best to distract the crowd of 5,000. My hula sisters and I formed a circle under the bleachers with Māpu, Kīhei, and Aunty Nana Kalama as the audience began to sing a song I don't remember. We held hands and talked about how we were feeling at that moment. After Māpu, Kīhei, and Aunty Nana left the circle to have a discussion of their own, my hula sisters and I decided that we did not want to dance. I remember being the one to tell Māpu that we were uncomfortable about performing and I remember the look of complete understanding and concern in her eyes. Māpu put our well-being above all else and was sensitive to our feelings. About an hour later the lights went on and the Festival resumed. When Hālau Mohala 'Ilima was introduced, Māpu went onto the stage and told the captive audience that we would not be performing that night because it would be inappropriate for us. She returned to our group and we could feel the strength of our conviction and the love all of us had for each other. It seemed as if the intensity of the chant was disrupted. For the first time that night, many of us finally felt peace.

After a brief moment, the next *hālau* was introduced and called to the stage. The dancers of Hālau Mohala 'Ilima were putting their costumes away. There was a light breeze blowing through the stadium and the rain was nothing but a soft mist. The storm had suddenly ended. The elements were calm.

A little boy left on a Maui beach late at night is all alone—except for . . .

Just Them, Passing Through

When I was a little kid many years ago on the island of Maui, where I grew up, I used to go fishing with my uncle and my dad, a lot. I was about eight or nine. It was quite a journey at that time, always at night.

My dad and uncle fished at one point on Honolua Bay and I would wait for them at Oneloa Bay. That's beyond Kapalua on the north shore of Maui on the road to Kahakuloa. Dad would leave me on the beach, make a little fire. My uncle would tell me, "Be still, stay there. Don't walk around. Sit down with your legs crossed."

I used to kind of wonder why.

Then one night we went fishing and Uncle left me at Oneloa Bay. He told me to sit still, no move, cross legs. So I sat there with my legs crossed, by myself, crying my heart out, wondering when they were coming back to get me.

Then I felt sand falling on my legs and I looked on both sides of where I was sitting on the beach and all I saw were huge footprints just appearing like a whole tribe came walking by. You know how sand kicks up when you walk? Well, it was kicking up behind the footprints and the sand was falling on me.

But I didn't see anything else. There was nothing

except huge footprints appearing and sand kicking up and landing on my feet. I didn't dare to move. I just sat still, my legs crossed, and the sand kept falling.

When Uncle came back I told him, and he said, "Oh, yeah, it's just them going down to the ocean. They're going back home."

"Who?" I asked.

"Oh, just them," Uncle said. "It's just them, passing through."

"But I no see 'um, just footprints and sand kicking up."

Uncle just smiled at me and said: "When you're older you'll know."

When I got older I found out that over there, that's where they found the *heiau* at Oneloa. My cousin, Anthony Kekona, was the one who took care of it. He was like the guardian. I found out who was passing through, but, funny thing, you know even now, all grown up, with a son, I live on O'ahu now, and I never go back there. No way.

Everyone needs directions
when traveling interisland,
as three Honolulu women
discover when they meet
an old Hawaiian man
in Kailua-Kona
Airport on . . .

A Moonless Night in Kona

It happened during Thanksgiving weekend, 1967, in Kona. I was working for a travel organization in Waikīkī. My job entailed offering recommendations to visitors on places to see, things to do, and hotels to stay in.

About three times a year, my two co-workers, Juanita and Aulani, and I would plan a trip to one of the neighbor islands over a long weekend to stay familiar with new hotels, tours, etc.

We had spent about two weeks planning our upcoming trip to the Big Island. Because of its size, we drew a map of the Big Island and marked all the places we would be stopping at around the island, figuring this would make it much easier for us once we were on the road.

Aulani and Juanita decided to make this a "fun trip" and asked their husbands to join us. As usual, airline reservations were tight: Juanita and I were able to get on a 5:00 P.M. flight to Kona, but we had to wait until approximately 9:00 P.M. for Aulani and the two husbands, who were arriving on a private plane.

Juanita and I sat in the old Kona airport talking and passing the time watching people come and go. I pulled our map out of my bag a couple of times to review some of the stops we'd be making. As darkness fell, the crowds thinned out. By 8:00 the final commercial flight had come and gone and workers were locking up for the night. An Aloha Airlines employee came up to see if we needed assistance; when we told him we were waiting for a private plane, he smiled and told us we were in the perfect spot since the private planes landed right outside.

After he left, I was spooked, because no one else was in the terminal! I decided to sit across from Juanita so she could watch my back and vice versa. It was eerie. The parking lot was pitch black, and the lights on the runway were dull and looked as if they were dancing. And the quiet—it was oh, so quiet. I kept looking at Juanita and she kept looking at me, both of us trying to put up a brave front!

I turned to the right and looked out onto the runway. It was a moonless night, the ocean was calm, and I could see the silhouette of a *kiawe* tree against the dark sky. I was mesmerized by this scene. Then a movement down by the *kiawe* tree caught my eye. I blinked to make sure I wasn't seeing things. Yup, there was movement down there. I could see figures walking along the shoreline at the edge of the runway.

Wait a minute! I could see men wearing *mahiole* and feather capes. They looked like warriors! There was no sound. It hit me like a lightning bolt! These were night marchers, a long procession of them. The hair on the back of my neck stood up. I was as white as a sheet! Juanita was trying to talk to me, and I kept telling her to be quiet, not to make a sound.

All the stories I had heard from my *tūtū* and my dad

came to mind. I kept pointing to the procession and telling Juanita about the movement, but she kept telling me there was nothing there. I don't know how she could have missed them.

I was quite shaken after this experience. Juanita and I were both scared. I sat completely still in my chair and would not look out at the runway. I was looking straight ahead and could see someone approaching, walking toward me. He was an older Hawaiian gentleman, slim, with white hair and dark skin, wearing a long-sleeved white shirt, a *lau hala* hat, and long pants. He was walking, but he wasn't making a sound. How can that be, I thought.

I was trying to tell Juanita that he was coming from behind her, but no sound would come out of my mouth. This gentleman walked right up to me and said, "Aloha." He had a dazzling smile.

I answered by saying, "Aloha, how are you?"

He said, "I came to get the map that you have in your purse." I was dumbfounded!

Juanita, in the meantime, asked him where he came from. He replied, "I come from Hilo and I have to get the map."

With that, I got the map out of my purse and handed it to him. He took it from my hand and thanked me. Juanita then asked him where he was going and he said, "I'm going back to Hilo." Then, he turned and began to walk away from me. He walked about ten feet and then disappeared into thin air!

This completely unraveled us! We didn't know where to turn or what to do because we were the only people at the airport. Soon we heard a plane approaching. When it landed, we ran to greet our friends.

Upon overhearing our story, an elderly Hawaiian woman walked up to me and told me not to fret. "Those night marchers were your *ʻohana*, welcoming you to the place of your family's beginnings. Don't fear them, embrace them, for they will watch over you during your stay here.

"As for the gentleman who took your map, he was your *ʻaumakua*, who took the form of a human. Danger was awaiting you at one of the sites marked on your map, and he was protecting you."

Having said that, she got into a car and drove off.

Often they gathered in
Kaʻaʻawa on Friday nights
at Honey's house on
Kamehameha Highway
across from the beach to sip
champagne, enjoy great
meals, and share good times.
Everything about those
evenings seemed wonderful,
except the long, dark ride
home from the country.
It all had something
to do with . . .

Uncle Eddie

Uncle Eddie was different. He married a lady from England and they had no children. They lived in Kaʻaʻawa across Kamehameha Highway from the beach. Next door in the three-home compound his sister, Aunty Lani, had her country home. Honey, the other sister and my grandmother, had her country home next door to Aunty Lani's. We went to the country home frequently as I grew up. Then, after Grandpa died and the freeway went through their property in Kaimukī, Honey moved to Kaʻaʻawa. Sometimes I visited her for a few days, and my cousin Anna stayed there while attending Church College, now Brigham Young University-Hawaiʻi.

But back to Uncle Eddie. He was well known in Kaʻaʻawa. He was always meeting someone, conferring, bringing out water and ti leaves and sprinkling them. He worked for the city auditor's office and would take the big Windward Taxi to and from work at City Hall in downtown Honolulu. Somehow, he'd get the weekly serials, the ones usually seen in movie theaters, like "The Shadow Knows" and others, all in black and white. So on Friday nights, everyone, or so it seemed, gathered at his large patio to enjoy the latest serials, shown using his ancient projector and a large sheet hung from the rafters. Sometimes he'd watch and sometimes not, for he'd be praying and such in another part of the house, sort of like a *kahuna* or something.

When I stayed over, Anna and I would drink champagne. She loved it. And so did Honey. Sometimes, we'd tease Honey, saying that we didn't want to invite Aunty and Uncle because they'd drink too much and leave less for us. Honey would lecture and we would recant, saying that we were just teasing.

One night Uncle Eddie and Aunty Alice came over and all us were going strong. We ate dinner at Honey's large dinner table and continued to consume champagne. Then, out of the blue, Uncle Eddie said to me, "I see the ghost of George Fern above your head."

I immediately felt a strange feeling up and down my back.

Honey said, "Don't be silly, Eddie!"

Well, I had heard the name before. George Fern was one of my grandfather's relatives, and he and his wife were childless and had wanted to adopt my father. I am named after my father, for I am Ellwood L. Fern, Jr.

Why would George Fern's ghost visit me—or was it Uncle Eddie's imagination? I had never felt that before, an instant chill up and down my spine that did not go away. I stood up and said, "Goodbye!" I left in my Volkswagen bug and headed home, although I was supposed to stay over at Honey's.

My car stalled at the top of the hill entering Kualoa. It stalled again in Hakipu'u. And again in Kahalu'u. I pushed the car each time and it started. At Hygienic Store, it stalled again. I turned and screamed, "Leave me alone!" I pushed, it started, I drove home to Kuliʻouʻou without another stall.

The next day I went to my regular service station and my car was thoroughly checked. Nothing was wrong, and it never stalled again in all the time I owned it.

I don't know how I escaped from George Fern's ghost. I never want to feel that chill or go through that again!

Although few people ever see Madame Pele, Roy Fujie has had three amazing encounters with the elusive fire goddess, twice on Lāna'i in the 1940s, and again in the late 1950s on the Big Island of Hawai'i, where she thanked him for a cigarette in her own volatile way.

Roy and Pele

In the early 1940s, Pele was seen on Lāna‘i by my husband, Roy Fujie. She was all in white and rode on a fiery horse with her white dog running beside it. She came down Ninth Avenue from the Hotel Lāna‘i area, crossed Lāna‘i Avenue and headed toward Fraser Avenue and the Catholic Church.

Roy heard the clippity-clop of the horse's hooves, but the horse with Pele and her dog seemed to fly or float through the air.

He had just finished his night shift at the power house there, so he thought he was just imagining all this in the early morning moonlight.

•••

In the late 1950s, Roy was the night shift supervisor (*luna*) for the pineapple pickers in the farthest fields to the southwest of Lāna‘i plantation when Pele again appeared. She was all in white, a little old lady with her white dog on the dirt road. Roy stopped his pickup truck to offer her a ride, but she only asked for a cigarette. So he reached into his glove compartment and got a fresh new cigarette and lit it with his own to give it to her. But she wasn't there when he offered it to her.

When there was a radio news report about the rumblings of an imminent eruption at Kīlauea Volcano, Roy went to visit his two brothers in Hilo and went to Halemaʻumaʻu crater. There was a boatload of tourists off the *Lurline* that morning at 9:30. They were all very disappointed because nothing was happening.

So Roy took a fresh cigarette from his shirt pocket, lit it and threw it into the caldera saying, "Here, Pele, you did not take the cigarette I offered you on Lānaʻi, so now please puff on this today."

Then in full confidence he told the tourists around him that Pele would surely erupt that night. To his great joy and luck, Pele did blow up that very evening at 9:30. The *Lurline* crowd came back to thank Roy, whom they recognized as the fellow in a *lau hala* hat with a *kolohala* feather lei who had offered Pele a cigarette and asked her to puff that day.

The Hawaiian word
mu'umu'u means "cut off,
shortened, amputated."
It's also the nickname of a
scary character who haunted
the "small-kid" days of
Maui youngsters, as
George Y. Fujita tells us in
his nostalgic,
prize-winning story.

Muʻumuʻu

Sometimes things happen and the events are etched so clearly in your mind that you will never forget the day. The Saturday I met Muʻumuʻu face to face would turn out that way for me.

"Yoshchan, come. I want you to buy mama some Lahaina *nasubi* today. I was going to ask Tetchan but she had to go to the library. You know what Lahaina *nasubi* is?"

"Yeah. That's the small-kine eggplant, right?"

"That's right. It's season time now. It's hard to get, so there's goin' to be plenty of people trying to buy. They'll be bringing them in on the Lahaina bus—the red and white one and it comes at eight. Okay?"

"I know, mom." My mom made the best *tsukemono* in town. Her pickles were better than my grandma's, and the purple *nasubi* ones were her specialty. Everyone knew that.

"I want you to wait for the bus, and as soon as they unload the vegetables I want you to get in line and buy me a dozen. Don't lose this money now. Can I trust you? . . ."

Market Street on Saturday is the smell of roasted peanuts, steamed pork in the *lau lau*, ginger leis, and ripe papayas. The *manapua* lady's tinkling bell and the tofu man's plaintive call of "Tofu, *aburage*. Tofu, *aburage*." And it's a no-school day. That Saturday I was pumped up to go.

After a while the Lahaina bus turned down Main Street and came into view. It was packed with people and all kinds of goods. Vegetables, mangoes, and even chickens tied up by the wings and kneeling down. Everybody who was waiting started to push and shove and this fat lady cut in front and pushed me aside like I wasn't there. Her eyes were so far away from her feet that she probably had no awareness of what was going on down below. By the time I got to the head of the line there were only two *nasubis* left. "Oh, well. You can't trust Yoshchan." I could already see the disappointment in my mother's face.

Everybody wears Saturday clothes on Saturday. But you can tell the locals from the country people because the country people wear *hoʻokano,* dressy clothes. This lady was definitely from the country because she wore a hat and fancy shoes and carried a large *kalakoa* bag. She seemed to be looking for someone. And she was walking straight toward me.

She was strangely exotic and strutted like the peacocks in the plantation manager's yard. She wore a bright *holokū* and walked like she owned the street. She swished by me, and the heavy smell of gardenia perfume enveloped me.

Just then, her bracelet fell off, but she kept on walking. As soon as I picked it up I was thinking, "Did she notice? Is she watching?" Since I couldn't muster up the guts to figure it out, I ran after her.

"Hey, lady! Hey! Ah, . . . you drop this?"

She turned abruptly and swept me with her eyes. "Well, sonny. My. My. For goodness sake. Thank you."

With a swoop, she deftly took the bracelet with one hand and held me with her other before I could withdraw mine. Again her heavy perfume descended on me. I felt woozy.

"Listen, sonny boy," she said, "do you know where Mr. Ambrose lives?"

I was befuddled and was doing my best to regain my composure. Meanwhile, inside of my head I was thinking, "Yeah, I know him, but nobody calls Mu'umu'u 'Mr. Ambrose,' and my name is not 'sonny.'"

Out loud, though, I found myself saying, "Mr. Ambrose? The ditch-man?"

Her head was nodding.

I should have shook my head and said, "No, I don't know."

Instead I found myself nodding just like her. "Yeah, I know where."

"Where?"

She had me nailed. I might as well have been handcuffed.

Still I tried, "He lives far away, you know."

Even as I said that, I knew it wasn't going to work and I was going to be late for the ball game at Mill Camp. I was scared shitless but I found myself walking in the general direction of Pi'ihana Camp. Toward Mu'umu'u's house. It was going to be a strange day for me.

I'll never forget the first time I saw Mu'umu'u. We were coming home from school when Joe asked, "Hey, you guys saw the man over there? He no more one hand."

"What you mean, 'no more one hand'?"

"No more."

"For real?"

"Let's go see!"

"No, you cannot just go look. He get one mean temper and a wild dog. But I tell you what. I show you guys how. You guys know how you make side eye?"

"What that, side eye?"

"Like this."

We all made side eye, but Joe said Jukichi didn't know how. "Come here, Jukichi. Stand by this mirror."

Standing there by the Coca Cola machine, Jukichi learned how to turn his eyes but not his head.

"Okay, you guys, no screw up now. I mean it. Mu'umu'u is one wild man and his dog is worse. Follow me."

Joe put his finger to his lips, turned, and circled the block so that we could go by Mu'umu'u again.

We did okay at first, but were so nervous we almost peed in our pants as we walked toward Mu'umu'u. But then Hippo began to giggle. And Jukichi forgot how to make side eye and began to weave down the narrow sidewalk. He stumbled and stepped on the tail of Mu'umu'u's dog. Then all hell broke loose. The dog barked and started chasing us. Joe was running hard and yelling, "Look out for Mu'umu'u!"

We ran so hard we beat the dog to the gate of the churchyard and slammed it shut. Then with Mu'umu'u cursing us kids we took off across the graveyard and took refuge in the garage.

Joe kept on saying, "You stupid bastard, Jukichi. You almost got us killed!" He slapped Jukichi on the head and we all sat down to catch our breath. Then Joe told us how Mu'umu'u lost his hand.

In the old days they built an irrigation system to bring water from East Maui to tap the Haleakalā watershed. Working their way through the mountains, the powder-men used dynamite to blast out tunnels.

These powder-men were special and different from the ordinary *dokata*-men who worked with picks and shovels. They were the ones who started the powder fishing. They threw dynamite into the water and after the big "boom," the fish would belly up and be easily picked up. They said that Mu'umu'u was number one at powder fishing and was even able to get *akule* sometimes. Joe said the trick was to be able to spot the fish as they swam around, and Mu'umu'u was the best.

The way the powder part works is that you "see" the fish, then light the stick of dynamite and throw it just in front of the school and blow them up.

Joe whispered to us that one day Mu'umu'u waited too long for the fish. . . . "Kaboom!" That was the story. After the accident, Mu'umu'u was given the job of ditch-man. Everybody called him ditch-man up front, but Mu'umu'u behind his back. His dogs were known to bite kids, and we weren't supposed to stare at his stump hidden in the sleeve of his chambray shirt. Everybody wondered what the stump looked like, but nobody knew. That was the Mu'umu'u secret.

Just as Joe got finished telling us about Mu'umu'u, the priest drove into the garage. Before we could escape, he asked us what we were doing there, and stupid Jukichi blurts, "Oh, we hiding from Mu'umu'u."

"Hiding? Why?"

We couldn't believe it. Jukichi got all scared of the

old priest and started to tell him everything. Soon we were in the rectory and the old priest was saying, "You boys did a real bad thing. God would want you to go to Muʻumuʻu right now and confess to him and apologize."

We all shook our heads. Who the hell would like to go back and talk to Muʻumuʻu?

"Well, then you must do penance. I want you all to close your eyes and pray with me and ask for God's forgiveness. And next Saturday morning early I want you all back here to help clean the yard."

As soon as we were out of earshot of the old priest, Jukichi got his head slapped for the second time. I thought Joe was going to kill him. What the hell did he have to tell the priest for? Just because he was wearing black clothes you don't have to tell him everything. "Jesus!"

By the time Saturday rolled around we had forgotten about the clean-up. That is, all of us except Jukichi. He showed up, and when his father found out about what he was up to, he gave him spankings.

But not long after, Jimmy got bit by his own dog. Bessie had never bitten anyone before, but almost as if there was a curse on us, she bit Jimmy's hand and he had to have stitches and all. And it was the right hand, just like Muʻumuʻu's!

Then another guy who was with us that day, Hippo, got an infection from a cut in his right hand, and Joe started to tell us that there was a curse on our heads because we didn't confess and do our penance. It was spooky. We were being cursed. One by one.

When Joe got his hand slammed in the car door, I became the only one left. But nothing happened to me—or so I thought.

Up close the country lady seemed more likable and less teacher-like. She had a pheasant lei in her *lau hala* hat, and her dress and exotic perfume all fit together. I couldn't quite figure out if she was a fun-lady or a mean boss-lady or what exactly had got me into nodding and going along with her.

By the time we reached the patch of tobacco growing near Camp One, she was sweating and her perfume was reeking and I felt like I couldn't breathe very well. I had tried three different versions in my mind of getting out of this, but each time I turned to look at her I knew it would be futile to try anything. So we kept on going. Past the chicken coop where I picked up a long feather that a fighting cock had lost from his tail, and over the hill toward the next camp.

Muʻumuʻu's dogs were a wild bunch, and when they got excited—well, they always got excited—they barked up a storm.

Soon I saw the mango tree by the mill, and as we neared Muʻumuʻu's house I began a serious search for a stick to ward off the dogs. But before I could find anything, the geese let the dogs know we were coming and the wild barking began. I was reaching for some rocks to throw at them when the lady walked right up to them and said, "Here, doggie . . . " and they started to act like puppies.

Holy moly. Is this magic?

"Tony! Tony?" she called. Then, "Anthony?" The door opened and Muʻumuʻu appeared. He looked disheveled, like we had woken him up, and instead of his usual faded chambray shirt with an empty sleeve, he was wearing a sleeveless undershirt. His stump was hanging out!

Had she not called out, if she had asked me if this was where Mr. Ambrose lived, I could have made my move. I could have said, "That's his house," and took off. Things were happening too fast for me.

Mu'umu'u said, "Aunty!" and ran up to her. He picked up her bag, and she took hold of me, and before I could catch my breath we were in Mu'umu'u's house. It was very neat and clean inside. The yard was a mess, but the house was washed-down spotless from being hosed down and wet mopped. There were the usual Catholic figurines hanging from the wall. Just inside the front door, leaning on the wall, was a twelve-gauge shotgun.

They were happy as hell. "Tony, I haven't seen you in three years."

"Really? That long."

I tried to collect my wits, and waited for the conversation to break and said, "I gotta go." My voice sounded funny. She would have none of it and pushed me down on a chair at the table. She searched in her bag and pulled out a well-laundered flour bag that was full of fixings for a lunch. The *pao doce* had that yeasty, sweet smell of just coming out of a stone oven, and she wouldn't listen to my plea that I had to go to the ball game.

Chewing on the bread, I watched her playing with her bracelets. It was spooky. She had a way of doing a twist with her fingers and wrist, and was dropping them on the table one by one. Right in front of me.

Then she gathered them up and slipped them back on her wrist. Just when I figured that she had deliberately "lost" one of them to seduce me into helping her, I looked up at her and she stared right back at me and did that twist drop, twist drop again. She was not only a witch, she was showing off her witchcraft to me. I was getting woozy again.

All along I had the feeling that I didn't belong where I was. Up close to Mu'umu'u with his stump hanging out right in front of me. This uneasy feeling kept getting worse, so I made several attempts to leave, but after the third try she made me feel like if I asked again she would be stomping mad.

She pulled out some old photographs and started telling me about how young Tony had come to Maui with his mom and dad from Portugal and how his mom died when his sister was born and how his dad died when he got kicked in the head by a mule.

She saw how jumpy I was, and so she reached over into her *kalakoa* bag and said, "Here, I want you to take this home to your mommy." It was a neatly woven basket made of coconut fronds.

I opened the cover and on the bottom I saw the Lahaina *nasubis*, all neatly lined up. I started to count them. Ten, eleven, twelve, thirteen. Thirteen *nasubis!* Now I knew she was a witch.

I was sitting right in front of Mu'umu'u, and his stump was pointing at me. I tried desperately not to look at it. But the more I tried not to look the more it followed me. Even when I looked away it followed me.

When he tore a piece of bread with both his "hands," I thought I lost it. The moment passed but I thought I heard myself gasp. Afterward I could not tell if a sound came out from my throat. I hoped nobody heard me if I did gasp. I looked toward the door and all I could see was the shotgun.

They kept on talking, but I was so scared I couldn't

make out what the conversation was about. I couldn't hear a word and I was choking from stuffing my mouth with bread.

Finally what I dreaded most happened. He was beckoning me. "Come sit by me."

And she was nodding her head again. Up and down, up and down.

I found myself standing and shuffling toward him.

"You like see this?" The stump was inches from me! And he was saying, "Go ahead touch if you like."

I was chicken skinned to the tip of my toes. Shaking, I looked up at his face.

He was smiling. "Try touch."

I reached up and it was warm, supple, and smooth. "WOW!"

Immigrants came to Hawai'i seeking fortune, opportunity and a better way of life. As years went by, their colorful stories were passed from generation to generation. From the days between the second and the third generation, Richard S. Fukushima recalls the story of . . .

Mamoru

Kenneth Mamoru Tanigawa lived a very simple life with his parents on the island of Kaua'i. His parents were plantation workers who worked for the pineapple cannery.

Mamoru-kun, as his parents called him, always enjoyed listening to stories his father heard at work from Native Hawaiians. The stories Mamoru liked best were ghost stories, which the Japanese called "obake."

Mamoru's mother used to teach him the Japanese beliefs about doing things correctly. She used to remind Mamoru that if he did something incorrectly, something would happen to him. One of the things Mamoru recalled was his mother telling him: "If you sleep with your hands upon your chest, you will have bad dreams." Mamoru, of course, did not believe it.

After Mamoru finished high school, he left home and went on to the university, but the stories his father told and the beliefs his mother taught remained in his subconscious. Mamoru studied hard and tried to better himself, because his parents had high aspirations for him. Upon graduation, he entered military service and served a tour of duty in Japan.

Mamoru enjoyed Japan, He was in the land of his

grandparents. He traveled the country and visited as many places as he could. After a year, Mamoru received a telegram from the American Red Cross. His father was seriously ill, and Mamoru was granted emergency leave to fly home to Hawai'i.

Mamoru was then placed on a C-120 military aircraft that flew from Japan to Wake Island, the first leg of the long trip back to Hawai'i, which took ten hours of flying time.

At Wake Island, there was a five-hour stopover. The crew of the aircraft, Mamoru, and another serviceman from Hawai'i who was also going home on emergency leave were billeted in the barracks for the five hours. Everyone took a nap after the long, exhausting flight from Japan.

Suddenly, Mamoru was awakened by a loud, strange noise telling him that his father was dead. Mamoru couldn't believe it, so he jumped up from the bed and looked around the room and saw that everyone was sleeping. Where did the voice come from and how did the voice know that Mamoru's father was dead? It puzzled Mamoru and he wanted to call home to Hawai'i from Wake Island to see if it was true. He found a telephone, but then decided not to call. He decided to wait until he reached Honolulu.

Five hours later, the crew was back on the airplane heading for Hawai'i from Wake Island. This trip was another ten-hour trip. Approaching Hawai'i, the plane flew over the island of Kaua'i. Looking out the window, Mamoru saw an unusual ring of clouds covering the island. Only the mountaintop could be seen from the plane.

When the plane landed at the Honolulu Airport,

Mamoru called his sister to pick him up. She told him that their father died. Mamoru asked what time, and learned that his father died at about the same time he heard the voice on Wake Island. However, Mamoru still could not believe it. The next day he flew back home to Kaua'i for the funeral.

The day of the wake, Mamoru went with his family to the mortuary to bring his father's body home. Following the hearse from the mortuary, Mamoru saw his father's face in the rear window of the hearse. He did not tell anyone, fearing that no one would believe him.

"Yes, Dad," he silently told himself, "I have come home to see you. May your soul rest in peace."

Sometimes when a person is dying they may urge family members to mend a broken relationship, patch up an old wound. In this poignant story, a Kaua'i man receives a message from his terminally ill niece in a dream, and heeds the last wishes of . . .

Sherry Lee

Family feuds happen in the best of families, and my family is no exception.

My brother Paul and I once had one of the closest brother-brother relationships that anyone could want. But in the late 1970s, we parted and went separate ways.

Paul was a career Army man, who traveled to Germany, Korea, Okinawa, and Stateside. He had a daughter named Sherry Lee, who was well aware of the relationship her father and I had. During Paul's tour in Aberdeen, Maryland, Sherry Lee was diagnosed with leukemia. I was not aware of Sherry Lee's medical condition, since I was not corresponding with Paul.

Paul was reassigned to Hawai'i and stationed at Fort Shafter. During that time, Sherry Lee was receiving chemotherapy at Tripler Army Medical Center.

On the morning of September 20, 1979, between 2:00 A.M. and 4:00 A.M., I did not know if I was awake or if I was dreaming, but I saw Sherry Lee descending from the sky, dressed in white. She looked like an angel, but she did not have any wings. She came closer and closer, and then stood next to my bedside and told me to "Please talk to my father. He really misses you, but does not know how to go about communicating with you again."

I said okay, I will try, and then Sherry Lee disappeared.

Later that morning, I called my family in Honolulu, to find out that Sherry Lee was at Tripler Army Medical Center and was not doing too well. I then called my mother and asked her if she wanted to go to Honolulu and see Sherry Lee the next day.

On September 21, 1979, my mom and I went to Honolulu and went straight to the hospital. To my shock and amazement, Sherry Lee was on a life support unit, bald, and lying almost lifeless on the bed. I could not believe the condition she was in. She was not like how I saw her in my dream.

Other family members were present, and someone said, "Let's all go to the other room and pray for Sherry Lee." Dumbfounded, I followed the rest of the family, and we held hands and formed a circle and prayed for her.

My nephew started praying for Sherry Lee's release from the pain that she was suffering. I was again in more shock. I did not expect to pray for Sherry Lee's release, but to pray for her to get better.

After the prayer, we went to see Sherry Lee in the other room. I watched in a trance as the lines on the monitor above her bed went from wavy lines to just a straight line—and then just a plain beep. Sherry Lee had died.

A nurse came in and disconnected all the wires and tubes from Sherry Lee's body and then covered her face with the sheet. The nurse expressed her sympathy and then left us standing there in awe. On September 26, five days later, Sherry Lee was laid to rest at Punchbowl Cemetery, the National Cemetery of the Pacific, under a little tree.

I recently visited Sherry Lee's gravesite and noticed that the little tree has grown and that it now shades her resting place. Last September was the twentieth anniversary of her death. May her soul rest in peace.

My brother Paul and I are at peace also.

Since the early '80s I have lived at the beach in Lanikai on Oʻahu's windward side, which enjoys one of the most agreeable, comfortable climates in the world. But, once or twice each year, the day holds its breath and the sun seems way too hot. Even people accustomed to living in the tropics complain. Everyone gets "dat burning feeling back of da eah." In Jeff Gere's story, it's not just the heat that's intense . . .

When Kona Winds Blow

Nobody had a story for me after my performance for seniors at Kailua Park. Darn. Unlocking my car door, I heard my name called hoarsely. A gaunt old Hawaiian man hurried toward me, wheezing and waving his hands.

"Oh, Mr. Gere, I SO enjoyed your talk, OH."

We shook hands. I mumbled something. His cloudy eyes gleamed, and he had a long turkey neck.

"I just HAD to come after you. SURE you're a busy guy, but betcha have a minute for a story. Yep, well PER-HAPS you know my SON? He's a VERY famous *kumu hula* here, Johnny Kalaniana'olealoha'āinaonaumaka . . . [on and on]."

"No, sorry, I don't."

"FAMOUS! . . . teaches the *keiki* an' *tūtū*, *kahiko* an' *'auwana*, EVERY-thing . . . goes to the Merrie Monarch an' all . . . his specialty is doing traditional chants that are new."

Curious. "How's that work?" I asked.

"Well, that's my story.

•••

"He was raised here in Kailua by my father and grandfather while my wife and I were working. My grandfather built the house. OH! what a view of Kāne'ohe Bay!
Now the mountainside is kinda STEEP, see, so he built
a rock wall foundation and the two-story house on top
of that. OH! you MUST come visit! Now they BOTH
spoke Hawaiian to the boy—the OLD Hawaiian. You
don't hear that too much anymore. So he grew up bilin-
gual, see? Now he and HIS family have the house.

"Well, one day we were cleaning up in the basement.
I was taking a box of junk out the double doors that face
Kona and I happened to look up. Above the door and on
the side with the rock bench the ceiling was burned
black! I turned an' said, 'Son, it's NO GOOD lighting a
fire under the HOUSE!' HEH! It's a joke, see, because
the roof of the basement is the floor of the HOUSE, see.
I gotta chuckle outta that.

"But my son looked up at me alarmed. 'What,
Daddy, I nevah tell you?'

" 'Tell me WHAT, son?'

" 'Oh, Daddy. Daddy, sit down.'

"He rubbed his chin a minute. 'A couple of times a
yeah, when da Kona winds blow, I get dis burning feeling behind my eah, an' I know she coming. I put da kids
an' wife in bed an' move all da fans down heah—da little ones in a circle, da tall ones wid da stands behind
dat. Den I wait . . . . I wait, 'cuz I know Madam Pele
gonna come an' visit me. *'Ae*, Daddy, Pele. Firs' come da
oli on da wind wit' tales of long ago—I wen chant 'em
all so many times . . . . An' me, I ansah wid praise fo'
Pele. Den I turn on da fans, 'cuz I know is gonna get
hot. She come in dat doah an sit wheah you stay, an' fo'
maybe fifteen minute she chant to me, *kahiko*, say what

she been doin' an' tinkin'. Dis fo' real, Daddy. I cannot believe I never tell you.'

" 'PELE? The fire goddess PELE?! This is fantastic! OH! But tell me: what does she LOOK like?'

" 'She big . . . maybe six foot seven, six foot eight . . . big bones, no fat . . . big ahms, big nose . . . deep brown skin, long black haiah flow wild down da back . . . and da eyes, Daddy, HER EYES! When she staht to chant, it staht getting hot, REAL hot, Daddy! Her eyes staht to glow red! Dull at firs', den hotter and brighter, like get one dimmah switch! Bright, den dull, up an' down. Big voice too! Ho, she shake da house! An' as she get into it, I stay heatin' up. Firs' my eyebrows an' da haiah on my ahm staht to wilt an' crinkle, like one dry leaf. Den come da sweat. I talking BUCKETS, Daddy! Sweatin' so much get one pool by my feet! One time I see green stuff—like pus—running off my fingahs! An' I squintin', 'cuz da *oli* stay burning me. Is like she reach right into my head, Daddy. Intense! Intense. I concentrate all I got on da *oli* 'cuz if I wen' lose 'em an' freak in da heat, I be flame an' go up like one match.'

"He snapped his fingers. *'Pau!'*

"He paused. 'Dat few minute seem like houahs.' He paused again. 'I tink she come 'cuz I undahstan' an' 'cuz I can take da heat. When she go I chant my aloha to her. An' every time, soon as she go, I fall down righ' in da middle o' da fans an' da goo. I mean, I done used up, spent already . . . every time.

" 'An every time, at dawn when da birds firs' burs' into song, me, I wake up. HO, I tell you! I wake up ALIVE, Daddy, really ALIVE! I giddy an' happy all ovah like one little kid! Is like I nevah seen cullahs befoah, like I nevah see my own house! I NEW! Every time! I rush upstaiahs quick to scribble da words o' da *oli*—scribble fas' 'cuz da chant is going off in my head! Oh, it come t'rough me clean, like rain outta da sky. An' I can see inside o' me how da hula gonna be, Daddy! Take sometime maybe two years fo' da *halau* to get 'um jes right. Gotta be PERFEC'! Den I show 'um. So dats why da ceiling stay black. Is 'cuz o' what happen wen da Kona winds blow an' I get dat burning feeling back of my eah.'"

He went away and I slumped in my car. The power of his tale settled into me and I started to cry. "My god! I've just heard how a prehistoric goddess continues to update her life story through a man living here, today, like I do. I'm so lucky I live Hawai'i. So, so lucky."

When Fox Lach was a
little girl, her grandmother
told her she had "the gift."
She didn't fully understand
what her grandmother
meant until
she inherited . . .

The Dark Mirror

It's a dark mirror. I am looking at it now. The glass of the mirror itself has a dark cast to it, but sometimes it seems dark in other ways. It is surrounded by an ornate, gold-carved frame. There once was a ribbon that lined the inside edge of the frame, but what remains are only moth-eaten shreds—a reminder of what used to be.

Not only is the mirror large, but it is heavy as well. I have no idea of its age; there are no hints or clues.

I am looking at it now.

●●●

The mirror has always held me spellbound, for it was my grandmother's before I inherited it. She was a small Filipino woman with what she called "the gift." She told me I've inherited that gift as well and, in time, would come to accept it fully.

I guess to her it seemed logical to bestow me with the mirror, one of the few belongings she brought with her from the Philippines. It hung in my grandmother's living room, and when I was a little girl it frightened and fascinated me. My mother said I had an overactive imagination. My grandmother clucked that she just didn't understand.

My grandmother said faces sometimes appeared in the mirror. Whose faces I do not know. When they came, strange things happened in my grandmother's house. She knew the faces and what could happen when they appeared. Sometimes, when the mean woman showed herself, doors opened and slammed shut and things were pushed from shelves. Another face belonged to a beautiful woman, richly dressed, and she seemed to enjoy making coffee cups rattle and clank together on their hooks behind closed cupboard doors.

●●●

As a child I never witnessed any of the faces or experienced the events. I only heard about them from my grandmother or from my parents, who always claimed there were logical explanations for such episodes. They didn't believe in my grandmother's mirror.

I would stand in front of the mirror for hours, hoping to see for myself, yet poised for flight if anything appeared.

●●●

A peculiar habit my grandmother had was to turn the mirror to face the wall at night before she went to bed. She never said why; she just did it.

My grandmother died at seventy-eight. She caught a cold while visiting us when we lived in Seattle, and she died the next day. Now, I've got the mirror. My granddad gave it to me twelve years after my grand-mother's passing. He said she wanted me to have it.

I hung my grandmother's mirror in my bathroom. I looked at the mirror every day but didn't see anything. And then it happened.

I've seen two faces. I think the first was the beautiful rich woman from an earlier time. I was brushing my teeth and as I turned to leave the bathroom I caught the reflection out of the corner of my eye. Our gazes locked. She smiled and vanished. I was left standing there, staring at my own reflection.

●●●

The second incident happened two days later. I walked into the bathroom looking for a hairbrush that sits in a basket below the mirror. The face that materialized was my grandmother's.

I don't know how long it was before I could catch my breath. It seemed stuck in my throat. She smiled and she mouthed the words, "Don't forget."

I think I nodded, because she nodded in return before she was gone. I knew what she meant without having to say more. I turned the mirror before going to bed that night, as I do every night now.

When a hitchhiker taps on Fox Lach's passenger window, she has a hunch it isn't any old woman she's picking up in . . .

Pele Goes Shopping in Kāneʻohe

Since my move to Hawaiʻi a few years ago I've heard plenty of accounts of Pele encounters but I never expected to have one of my own. My own background is steeped in a cultural sense of the spiritual, so when it happened on the windward side of Oʻahu I reacted not with fright but surprise and respect.

It was approximately 9:30 P.M., one Wednesday night in April 2001. I was dropping a friend off from work. After leaving him at his house I pulled up to the stop sign at Mikiola Drive and Kāneʻohe Bay Drive. I checked for traffic both ways, and seeing none I checked to my right again. I was startled to see an old woman with long gray hair standing on the corner under the plumeria tree. She was dressed in a long white *muʻumuʻu*.

I knew she wasn't there last I looked, so when she approached my car I already had the thought of Pele in my head. She tapped on my window, and I rolled it down and asked if I could help her.

She asked me to give her a ride to Kāneʻohe Bay Market. I didn't hesitate, even though I knew the market wasn't even half a block away.

When she got in the car she didn't say much, but I

was hit with the smell of pungent earth. I wasn't scared, just a little in awe, and wondering if this was really Pele.

She instructed me to drive around from the back side so I could pull right up in front of the doors to let her out. When she got out of the car and closed the door, I turned to watch her go in. She simply vanished. I knew she couldn't have walked in that quickly.

I couldn't restrain myself from going inside to look for her. The clerk looked at me as if I was a little off—nobody else was in the market—so I didn't bother to explain.

Every time I pass there I always look for that woman in white, just in case she needs a ride.

When Pele visits mortals, she usually tests their generosity by asking for food, drink, or a ride to another part of the island. When she visited Dwynn Kamai's "Moloka'i Grandma," however, she had something to share.

Pele's Birth Announcement

Agnes Kamai Yuen, "Moloka'i Grandma" as we affectionately knew her, was a tiny but very strong woman. Grandma was a jack of all trades and master of most. She worked at the state hospital and was an educator, award-winning artist, mother of eight, and grandmother of many.

At the time of this tale, the family had been living in Waiākea on the Big Island. You see, Grandpa Kamai was a heavy equipment operator, and many times had to uproot the family to go where the company sent him. Grandma had already raised three children and was *hāpai* with the fourth.

One day, as Grandma was walking down the trail on one of her frequent visits to the volcanoes, she was approached by a mysterious older woman dressed in white. She had long salt-and-pepper hair, and with her was a white dog. As the two met, the woman stopped Grandma and told her that she would deliver a boy and on that same day the volcano would erupt.

On July 1, 1931, Moloka'i Grandma delivered my father, Heine Kamai (her only son) and yes, that volcano erupted. We have always teased Dad that Hawai'i celebrated his birth with the natural fireworks of the volcano.

Madame Pele, as we believe the woman in the story to have been, visits as a young, beautiful woman as well as an older, mysterious woman. My family has encountered her in both versions.

Moloka'i Grandma and Dad are gone now, but their legacies live on.

Hawai'i welcomed the young California couple with open arms in the late '70s. Their first two years were filled with making their new Olomana house, in the hills above Kailua on O'ahu's windward side, a home. They worked on the successful development of their small remodeling business and supported their young son as he found his place at Maunawili Elementary School. They considered their move to Hawai'i a good one, and found that their normal flow of good luck and good times seemed to flourish in their new home. And then the flow shifted at . . .

Hale o Olomana

We were lying in bed reading late one evening when the first evidence of the shift was felt, literally. Jerry was distracted from his book by a gradual awareness of pressure on the lower part of his legs. He became conscious of an invisible presence sitting there, holding his legs firmly to the bed. Fearful and uncomfortable, in his "handle the situation" way he told the presence to leave.

Immediately afterward, he found the event hard to reconcile with his "Archie Bunker" attitude that spirit stuff is fluff, yet the episode was so real to him he had to admit that it really did happen. He took a deep breath and told Debby what happened. As she listened, she knew something must be giving them a message.

And so we began an examination of recent events in our lives. Were they somehow related to this "visit"? Debby had been in a serious accident, totaling her car, and the neighbor's toddler had tragically drowned in their pool. There was also an underlying, hard-to-define sense of imbalance and lack of control, and a feeling that the walls of the house had become cold. We were no longer enjoying the warm, welcoming home we cherish. The good luck and good times were not rolling so easily, and a general sense of dissatisfaction settled upon us.

We began to wonder whether the stories we were hearing about the spirituality of Mt. Olomana, the tri-peaked mountain that rose nearly out of our backyard, might have a bearing upon our experiences. We were told of spirits, unsettled and unready to move into the afterlife, who, in their confusion, played pranksterlike tricks on the current inhabitants at the base of their mountain. Were we now subjects of these tricksters? Had we somehow gotten in their way? Was it time to have our house blessed, as we had heard was the custom? We asked these questions of ourselves as we went on with our busy lives, but with a continuing sense of unrest.

●●●

As happens when we underestimate the lessons presented to us, the message was made clear in the middle of one gruesome night. We were awakened by the sounds of crunching and snapping directly outside our bedroom window. At first we thought it was just ʻEle ʻEle Nani, our trusty black lab, chewing on a bone or a ball or whatever else she might have found. But something about the persistence of the sound prompted Jerry to go outside and investigate. He was surprised to see a large brindle pit bull standing under our window. The powerful dog met his gaze with deep yellow eyes as it slowly backed across the yard and out through the open gate. This was disconcerting, since dogs do not typically hold eye contact with humans. It also seemed strange that the gate was wide open, since our wood shop was in the carport and we were quite careful about closing the gate at night. ʻEle ʻEle Nani watched the drama with her usual calm acceptance; she was a gentle dog, but it seemed odd that she would have let this strange dog into the yard.

Jerry was shaken, with a churning of primal fear in his stomach. But curious as to what the dog had been chewing, he returned to the area of the yard outside the window. Another shock met him head on: he found the remains of our son's two pet rabbits. Their cage had been ripped apart by the pit bull.

Though telling our son, Walker, that his rabbits were dead was difficult, it was even more difficult to face the possibility that we really might need some help dealing with the events being presented to us. We called a Hawaiian friend who we knew was connected to a *kahuna* lineage. She agreed to call her aunty, who performed blessings. After hearing only a few words about the spiritual visitations, Aunty asked, "Have the spirits yet sat on their legs?" She advised us, through our friend, to deal with the situation immediately, since next the spirit would sit on the chest or face, causing a suffocating feeling.

She offered to bless our house in such a way that the spirits would no longer be able to move through our space. We were reluctant to have this type of exorcism, since we wanted to share our home, not keep anyone, human or spirit, from passing through. We have always felt, especially in Hawaiʻi, that we are visitors upon this land, with no rights to exclusivity.

Jerry decided he would climb Mt. Olomana and meet whatever needed to be met. In doing this, he was grappling with his skeptic's role, relaxing his practical belief system enough to accept the possibility of the unknown. He was nervous about this change, but little did he know the test to which he was to be put.

•••

As a family we had all played on Olomana Peak and hiked other local trails. We had learned to leave a blessing of ti leaf and stone to show reverence to the beauty and peace surrounding and within us. Early in the morning, Jerry picked ti from our backyard, under our bedroom window. As the sky began to brighten in the east, he and 'Ele 'Ele Nani headed out across the well-worn path through the pastures leading to the mountain trail. They followed the fence line, moving with surety along the often-trekked trail.

Suddenly, Jerry found himself disoriented. He was no longer near the fence, and he wasn't where the trail started up the mountain ridge. He climbed a tree to see if he could get his bearings and found that he was nearly a quarter mile from the fence line. He climbed down and crossed to where he was able to pick up the mountain trail as it headed over the saddle to the ridge line.

As he headed up the hill, he stopped to collect rocks to add to his ti leaves as blessings. He chose a rock for each member of his family: one for Debby, one for Walker, and last, one for himself. As he placed his rocks in the backpack, he was suddenly weighed down by what seemed a hundred pounds.

This was almost too much for him to bear. He thought perhaps he was losing his mind. He took deep breaths and realized that even if it was all in his mind he needed to continue, to persevere through the challenges presented.

The sun rose majestically as he made his way up the narrow ridge of Olomana with his gift of ti and stone for the house and each member of his family. Morning bloomed. He reached the point of the trail where the other peaks of the mountain come into view, a place he had been many times. This morning those peaks rose up in a new splendor, revealing a power he had never before felt. As he gazed with a startled vision at the mountain, the wind became more than wind; he felt a touch upon his cheeks that could only be described as spiritual and intended.

His fear became more intense, accompanied by a determination to follow the path to its end. The next challenge, physical this time, took place where the path becomes a perpendicular cliff with cables to assist climbers to the next level. At this point he told 'Ele 'Ele Nani to stay below, and with a fear he had never before felt at the cables, and a determination beyond any he had ever known, he bested the perpendicular and shakily made it to the top of the peak. He emptied his backpack of a water bottle, an orange, three rocks, and three ti leaves. Looking out across the early morning light bathing Kailua and its bay, he felt a great sense of accomplishment and wondered whether this really was a trial or insanity.

But finish he must, so he picked up Walker's rock, rolled it up in the ti leaf, and knotted the stem. As he held it in his hands, he saw Walker playing in his room with friends. Sunlight was pouring in all the windows, making the room a warm and inviting cocoon.

After placing Walker's blessing in a safe crevice, he

wrapped ti around the rock for Debby. He then envisioned her standing at our front door in a *holokū* gown, welcoming guests into their home. Sunlight poured in the front door, with Debby standing in its rays. As gatekeeper, she held the power to bring in the light. He found a spot for her blessing and placed it tenderly.

Wrapping his own rock, Jerry tried to see himself in their home, but the vision changed. He found himself in the ocean, held by the ocean, as by a mother's arms. Having spent most of his life in or on the ocean, he was suffused by a feeling of comfort and safety. So he placed his blessing with his family's and was ready for the descent. The trip down the mountain was unencumbered. He met 'Ele 'Ele Nani waiting for him below the cables, and they romped their way down, relishing the freedom of a challenge well met.

•••

While Jerry was on his trek, Debby, nervous about their ordeal, decided to take a walk. Passing a house on one of the streets in the neighborhood, she saw a pit bull tied in a carport. Not having seen the dog when he so violently visited their yard, she hesitated to confront the owners until Jerry could identify it. Upon Jerry's return, they walked down the street to the house. The dog was not there. The owners said there had never been a pit bull tied in their carport.

Walker came home from school in the afternoon. Upon entering the house, he commented that it felt brighter and more open, and that the walls felt warmer. In the following weeks, friends asked if we had painted, rearranged furniture, put up new pictures. No, we had not, but the warmth of our home had returned along with the flow of good luck and good times. We had learned a new respect for the possible powers that feed the flow.

The bloody battle for Oʻahu by Kamehameha the Great in 1795 came back to life one night not so long ago when a Honolulu bus driver paused on the Pali Highway at the end of his shift and heard warriors "fighting, yelling, and dying." A young boy recalls this vivid story often told to him in . . .

My Grandfather's Ghosts

Well, I'm twelve years old and I happen to believe in ghosts and I'll tell you why: It's all because of my grandfather (who, by the way, is a big, brave, strong man). He's six foot two and I don't think he was ever afraid of ghosts. Until one night, long ago.

When I was four or five my mother told me the story about my grandfather and the ghosts of the Pali Highway, a story that didn't make sense then, but later, when I was six or seven, it really started to register and come into focus. This is how the story goes:

My grandfather was a bus driver and he was driving the Old Pali Road route one night, in spring or summer around 1956. He had already dropped off all his passengers and he was the only one on the bus.

It was just before midnight and he had turned off the bus, relaxing and waiting for his last run to start back down the hill to Honolulu. He was waiting for midnight so he could end his shift. All the bus drivers did this to keep on schedule.

Suddenly, he heard a lot of noise. It sounded like some kind of fighting was going on. He heard yelling and it got louder and closer. Next, he heard the clashing of what sounded like wood spears and clubs and men screaming in agony. It was like a war. Bam! bam!

As the sound came closer and closer my grandfather's bus started to shake like somebody mad was pushing it around, rocking it, and the trees were getting blown all over the place.

It's always windy up there, but this wasn't a normal gust of wind. This was something else. Then, all the sound and commotion came so close to my grandfather he began to believe that men were really fighting, yelling and dying.

When it sounded too real, he decided to get out of there as fast as he could and zoomed back to the bus depot. He was really frightened by it all. Just sitting up there even at daytime, to me, it's kind of scary with the wind and all.

My grandfather went to the dispatcher and told him what he had heard and felt up there on the Pali.

"We can put you on another route if you want," the dispatcher told my grandfather. And he agreed on the spot.

Next morning, he was told by some of the other drivers that they, too, had heard these noises in the past and asked to be transferred.

The Old Pali Highway route that my grandfather and others drove in those days was the same way that King Kamehameha had taken when he came to fight Chief Kalanikupule of Oʻahu.

The famous Battle of Nuʻuanu happened in April 1795, when Kamehameha's warriors fought Kalanikupule's. Some of Kalanikupule's warriors were driven over the *pali* (cliff) at the end of this valley.

Now, it seems that at certain times, usually around

midnight, people traveling alone on this Nuʻuanu route have experienced hearing these spirits fighting their way up the Old Pali Road.

Whenever I travel that road, today, I always keep my eyes peeled for the ghosts of the warriors of Kamehameha and Kalanikupule. I'm sure they are there. So is my grandfather. I wouldn't take a hundred dollars to spend the night up there alone. So keep your eyes peeled, too, when you cross the Pali alone at midnight.

A gift to Hawai'i's last
reigning monarch, the piano
made in New York from
Big Island *koa* wood was
presented to Queen
Lili'uokalani in 'Iolani
Palace on her fifty-third
birthday more than
one hundred years ago.
You can see the piano today
in Honolulu's Washington
Place, where Aunty Lei
discovered that something
wasn't right about . . .

A Piano for Lili'u

It was a beautiful morning! The sun was shining and my mother and aunt were looking forward to visiting Washington Place. They were to visit the home that my mom's great-great grandfather Isaac Hart built for John Dominis many years ago.

We are 'ohana (family) to Lili'u, and it is always a joy to visit the beautiful home that the governor of Hawai'i now resides in.

Mom and Aunty Lei checked in at the front and were waiting for a guide to come and take them on a tour of Lili'u's home. They had gone into the portrait room, where life-sized portraits of King Kalākaua and Queen Lili'uokalani dominate the room. Mom was standing in front of Kalākaua, and Aunty Lei was looking at the portrait of Lili'u. They were both thinking about the king and queen and how it must have been when they were alive. It was as if they were communicating with them somehow through the ages.

Continuing into another portion of the house, they came to a group of children standing in front of a grand piano. Someone in the group asked if anyone could play, and since my aunt is an accomplished piano player, she volunteered. Aunty sat at Lili'u's piano and started to play, but the sounds coming out of the piano were very strange. My aunt looked puzzled and started again. The music was deep and low, with a heavy bass sound. Mom asked my aunt what was wrong and my aunt said, "I'm not sure. These heavy sounds are the only ones coming out. I feel a very strong masculine presence here." She started again, and again the sounds were deep and heavy.

Mom said, "I've never heard you play like this before, Lei. What's going on?"

Aunty Lei said, "I don't know. I can't figure it out! It's as though Lili'u is trying to tell me something. I keep feeling a heavy masculine energy. I wonder why?"

After one more attempt, my aunt gave up, saying that this was the first time she was unable to play a piano. (Aunty Lei started playing the piano at the age of seven and has been a mentor for students from time to time.) She stood up and they walked away and waited for their guide.

The docent soon came to take them on their tour of Washington Place. They couldn't shake their strange experience with the piano, but tried to enjoy the tour anyway. When the docent came to the piano, she told its story:

●●●

Lili'u had been given the piano on the evening of May 12, 1892. It was presented to her in the throne room of the palace. The presentation "was made by Messers, [sic] John Phillips, J. H. Soper, and J. F. Hackfeld, the committee appointed for that purpose."[1]

The piano was a gift for Lili'uokalani's fifty-third

birthday, and it was intended to be "as Hawaiian as possible."[2] A huge *koa* tree from the island of Hawai'i was cut and shipped to the J. & C. Fischer piano company of New York.[3]

The interesting note here is that some of the group that presented the piano to Lili'u were instrumental in the overthrow of the Hawaiian monarchy in January, 1893.

John Harris Soper, who was born in Plymouth, England, came to Hawai'i in 1877. He began a career here, raising sugar, and was the manager of the Pioneer Mill in Lahaina, Maui. He was the head of the force that suppressed the Robert Wilcox rebellion of 1889. Soper was also asked to head the forces of the Provisional Government and it was under his command that the monarchy was overthrown. In January, 1894, he was commissioned as general in the National Guard, and he also suppressed the counterrevolution of 1895.[4]

Heinrich Hackfeld was born in Oldenburg, Germany, and came to Hawai'i around 1848. He developed a business of importing machinery and supplies for the sugar plantations and exported raw sugar.[5]

Many of the men who decided to have this beautiful piano made for the queen were the business elite or known to be sympathetic to them. It is interesting that they would have given Lili'u such a gift to gain her confidence when shortly thereafter they were plotting her overthrow.

● ● ●

After hearing this story on the history of Lili'u's piano, Aunty Lei turned to my mother and said, "That's it! That's why I felt the masculine energy. That's why I was feeling a sadness surrounding the piano. Lili'u doesn't like this piano. She does not want it in her home. Was this a gift of love? I know now that she was trying to tell me that she is not comfortable with this piano here."

Now everything became very clear. Hawaiians call this *puka mai,* "to make clear " or "to make known." Some of the men who gave Lili'u the piano were the ones who eventually overthrew her monarchy. Mom and Aunty Lei stood there looking at each other, wondering what to do.

That's where I come in. When they first told me this story, we knew that Lili'u's spirit was trying to get her message across. I know that she must trust my mother and my aunt very much. Maybe because we all are family. Maybe because Aunty Lei is very spiritual. Whatever her reason, I feel that she wants this story told.

I'm not sure how you feel about spirits, but I do believe they exist. I have had personal experiences that would be considered in the realm of the supernatural. Because things are unexplainable, does not mean they didn't happen. Because we can't see something, does not mean it doesn't exist.

When I spoke to Aunty Lei recently she said, "I know some people will not believe this. That's okay. Your mother was there to witness what happened, and I know that I do not want to ever play that piano again."

[1] "A Royal Piano," *Daily Pacific Commercial Advertiser*, p. 6.
[2] "A Royal Piano," p. 6.
[3] "Queen Lili'uokalani's Piano Will Be Sent to San Francisco to Be Shown at Diamond Jubilee," *The Honolulu Advertiser*, 14 June 1925, p. 8.
[4] Day, A. Grove, *History Makers of Hawaii*, Honolulu: Mutual Publishing, 1978.
[5] Day, *History Makers of Hawaii*.

When seven Hawaiians reburied the last of a thousand and more bones of their ancestors unearthed during groundbreaking for a new resort hotel at Honokahua, Maui, in 1991, they experienced a spiritual and inspiring encounter unlikely to occur again, as one member of the burial party explains in . . .

Ka Hō'ailona
(The Sign)

The modern-day name for the uninhabited island seen off the coast of Wailea, Maui, is Kaho'olawe, though our chants tell us that its ancient name was Kanaloa. Kanaloa was a primordial god from antiquities, and was the deity for the ocean, its animals, fresh water, salt water, and all the growth on Earth and in the sea. On the northwest side of Kaho'olawe is Ahupū Bay, whose west point is called Lae o Nā Koholā, or Cape of Whales.

The *koholā* (whale) was well known to the early Hawaiians. In the Kumulipo chant—the Hawaiian chant of creation—the Second Era speaks of the birth of the whale: *"Hānau ka palaoa noho i kai"*—born is the whale living in the ocean. And the *paukā*, or poetic passages, address the familiar scene in native Hawaiian culture of whales parading through the 'Alalākeiki Channel between Maui and Kaho'olawe.

This seasonal phenomenon reminds us constantly that from the time of our native Hawaiian ancestral migration, Kanaloa and his many ocean forms were continuously associated with the island Kanaloa.

The whale is the largest ocean form, and a majestic manifestation of Kanaloa. From the ivory of this creature, the highly prized *niho palaoa* was worn by the *ali'i* (chiefs) of high rank. The scarcity and beauty of the *niho lei palaoa* and its connection to Kanaloa brought *mana* (spiritual power) to the carver, to the pendant itself, and eventually to the wearer of the pendant.

The *ali'i* who possessed the *kino lau*, or body form, of this great god would themselves acquire the characteristics, intelligence, and knowledge of the god. Therefore, it would be advantageous for any *ali'i* to secure the ivory whale tooth of this Kanaloa body form.

The *koholā* is revered in modern-day Hawai'i not only by the thousands of whale watchers, but by the native Hawaiians, who still consider it as one of Kanaloa's magnificent creations.

In 1990, I was one of the fortunate ones who were touched by the *koholā*. Several of us were involved in relocating the Ritz-Carlton Hotel in Honokahua. Originally, the hotel was supposed to be built over ancient Hawaiian burial grounds. After strong objections from the Hawaiian community, it was relocated to its present site.

I was one of seven people chosen to rewrap the thousands of remains that had been dug up. The remains dated between A.D. 850 and the early 1800s. There were numerous *niho lei palaoa* (whale tooth necklaces), from one to six inches in length. This would indicate that royalty of all ages were interred with their symbols of nobility.

In 1991 a very spiritual incident occurred on the last night that we buried the last remains at Honokahua. At midnight, we were ready to start our burial rituals when we heard a loud slapping coming from Honokahua Bay.

As we looked over the hill into the bay we saw an outline of a whale lying on its side, rhythmically hitting the water with its pectoral fin. After about fifteen minutes it stopped, and we went back to the burial pit.

As we started our ceremonies, several owls flew overhead and screamed, then headed for the mountains. This was the Hōʻailona, the sign that our *kūpuna* were back reunited with their *iwi*, bones.

While the burials were taking place, a song came to me, which tells of the night's events. The name of the song is "Ka Hōʻailona" (the sign), recorded by the Pandanus Club in 1992, from the compact disc called "Te Tama."

In English it says:

> At midnight the conches blew as one
> Summoning the spirits back
> With the flames from the torches as a guide
> They came from the heavens above
>
> They came from Tahiti and Aoetealoa (New Zealand)
> To continue their eternal rest
> And again reunite with their bones
> In this land called Honokahua
>
> They did not know how to thank these men
> Who laid their bones to rest
> So they called upon the *koholā*
> Who slapped the waters of the bay
>
> In view was an owl, indeed it is a sign
> Their presence are here our great ancestors

Inhaled was their fragrance, by the
Beautiful blossoms, today's people
In Honokahua, yes the adornment of Maui

We will always remember
The place of my birth
Where the sign was given
that our *kūpuna* (ancestors) are at rest.

From black sand beach to its red dirt canyon rim, the Big Island's lush green Waipiʻo Valley sweeps back six miles between 2,000-foot-high cliffs laced by 1,200-foot-high Hiʻilawe Falls. The "valley of kings," once the political and religious center of Hawaiʻi, is steeped in myth and legend (here Māui was dashed against the rocks by Kanaloa) and full of the bones of old Hawaiian chiefs, maybe even those of Līloa and Lono. When helicopter pilots spot new caves in the sheer cliffs, they alert the Bishop Museum, which sends out an intrepid archaeologist who sometimes discovers that something beyond bones remains to be seen in . . .

Cliffside Burial Caves of Waipi'o Valley

Waipi'o is a delightful place to explore. You can hike down and up. For backpackers, the trail up the opposite side of the valley just back of the beach goes atop the cliff to Waimanu Valley. This all-day hike takes some preparation. Please, let someone know where you are and the days you will be gone, and arrange with them to notify the Fire Department Rescue Squad if you do not return on time. The rescue squad logs more calls here than anywhere else.

And now for my Waipi'o story. One week about thirty-five years ago we had a medium-sized earthquake centered near Waipi'o Valley. Several landslides occurred in the valley and along the shore-side cliffs. The next day a helicopter pilot flying along the cliffs reported that a landslide had opened the mouth of a formerly sealed cave. The pilot reported to Bishop Museum in Honolulu that he looked into the mouth of the cave and saw a large stack of human bones. Hawaiiana researchers at the museum keep a master map of the islands with all the important finds marked on it. This cave was something new. They sent over an archaeologist to investigate.

A cliffside burial cave. The problem was getting to

the cave. The opening was midway up the face of a 1,200-foot cliff with the ocean crashing at its base. The museum solicited my help and that of a helicopter. The helicopter transported six of us to the cliff's edge along with rope and pulleys. As the helicopter hovered beyond the cave's opening, so we could judge its location from above, we lowered the archaeologist down. He had a sketch book and a flashlight. Several hours later he tugged on the rope to signal that he was finished and wanted to be hauled up.

It's one thing to let someone down on a rope, but quite another to haul him back up. It took us all the rest of the day to haul him up foot by foot. The researcher concluded that the site was a burial cave of a major chief, who along with his warriors had died in battle before white men came to Hawai'i. The chief was laid out on a *heiau* of rocks within the cave. Bodies of his warriors had been stacked at the opening of the cave.

The interesting part was how the burials had been accomplished in such an impossible place high on the face of a perpendicular cliff. Found inside the mouth of the cave was a tree trunk with a hole bored through one end. Apparently, skilled climbers had scaled the cliff, then hauled the tree trunk up on a line. They anchored one end of the tree in the cave, and sticking the other end out in the air, used it as a boom to haul up the bodies.

There was also a spooky mystery about the cave. The archaeologist could not complete his investigation. He said his flashlight stopped functioning when he tried to go deeper into the cave.

In old Hilo town three generations ago, the Japanese grocer Sanzuchi Kaneshige encounters the spirits of Chinese workers who died building a bridge across a swift river.

Hitodama

My grandparents, who were immigrants from Japan, operated a small general store outside of Hilo soon after the turn of the century. One day, my grandfather went to town on his horse-drawn carriage.

By the time he finished the business in town, it was already quite dark. As he was hurriedly making his way home, his horse suddenly stopped and neighed as if frightened by something in the middle of a tall wooden bridge. Try as he might, he could not make his horse move.

This was a bridge that spanned a deep gorge and a swift river. He had heard that, many years prior to this, Chinese immigrant laborers had slaved under dire circumstances to build this bridge. He had heard that many laborers had lost their lives in the process of building this bridge. This was the infamous bridge built by the sweat and tears of early Chinese immigrants.

Just as he was remembering this story told to him by the old-timers, there suddenly appeared before him several eerie bluish-colored balls of fire floating in the air around him. He knew that these must be the *hitodama*, or balls of dead sprits, that he had heard of before.

Although he was almost frightened out of his wits, he closed his eyes tightly and managed to recite over and over again the Buddhist incantation "Namu Amida Butsu, Namu Amida Butsu, Namu Amida Butsu" ("Hail Amida Buddha, Hail Amida Buddha, Hail Amida Buddha").

Although it seemed like an eternity, he prayed and recited the incantation for only five to ten minutes. Finally, when he slowly and fearfully opened his eyes, the *hitodama* had disappeared without a trace. At the same time, the horse slowly started to walk forward again.

In this way, my grandfather was released from the stranglehold of the dead spirits and managed to safely return home to his wife and his many little children, including my father.

I believe that, more than the divine intervention of Amida Buddha or the power of the incantation, the thing that perhaps ultimately pacified the dead spirits was the compassion and the sympathy my grandfather, also an immigrant, felt toward the dead who died unfulfilled and angry at not being able to make the long-sought American dream come true.

Not too long after this incident, my grandfather closed down his store and moved to the north shore of Oʻahu with his growing family. After all, as the head of the household his primary responsibility was the safety of his family.

After two decades of searching cemeteries, Nanette Napoleon has only one real-life chicken skin story. It's a good one. While researching graves on O'ahu's Wai'anae coast, she agreed to meet a man named Wayne Davis who offered to show her . . .

Old Hawaiian Graveyards

We made a date to meet on a Sunday morning at eight o'clock at Tanouye's, the landmark drive-in on the leeward side. He described himself and I described myself. He said he was a big Hawaiian guy. So on a Sunday morning at eight o'clock I drove up and saw a big Hawaiian guy by himself at the outdoor seating area at Tanouye's.

"Hi, I'm Nanette Purnell. Are you Wayne Davis?"

He said he was and I sat down and started talking story, just chatting you know about this and that.

And then we went driving around in my car for three hours and we visited about twelve different graveyards, many I had never seen before—in the backs of valleys, and really out-of-the-way places. He was terrific; he really knew where to find the old Hawaiian graveyards.

We did this for three hours and I got back to Tanouye's and dropped him off.

The next day I was writing a thank-you note and I got a phone call. I picked it up and this man's voice said, "Nanette, this is Wayne Davis."

"Oh, Wayne," I said, "thank you again for taking me around. I really enjoyed it and I learned a lot."

And he said, "What are you talking about?" And then he said, "Where were you yesterday?"

"Wayne," I said, "Are you trying to pull my leg?" I thought he was making a joke. All of a sudden it hit me, and I started getting chicken skin on my arms, and I said, "Wait a minute. I'm confused. Wayne, did you go with me yesterday?"

He said, "No, I went there and waited for more than an hour and nobody showed up."

Then the hair on my neck stood up. I literally got chicken skin up and down my spine and I got scared.

"Wayne, don't joke with me, this isn't funny. I went there, at 8 o'clock, and met a man who said he was Wayne Davis and he got in my car and he took me to all the graves for three hours."

"Nanette, I don't know how to tell you this, but that wasn't me."

It wasn't funny to me now. "Were you there or not?" I demanded.

"I wasn't there," he said. "I called because I just wanted to find out what happened to you."

He said he arrived late for our appointment and waited, but I never showed up so he went home.

I still don't know who took me around, and it really bothered me, so about a month later I talked to this *kupuna* and told her the story and she told me to think of it this way, that maybe the ancestors were calling on me, sort of like an *'aumakua*.

"The old Hawaiians wanted you to know where they are," she said. After that I felt good about it.

Several months later, at a function, I saw a man with a name tag that read "Hi, I'm Wayne Davis," and

I introduced myself. It was the real Wayne Davis, all right, at least he said he was.

And, are you ready for this? He wasn't the same one who took me around the old graveyards.

Progress always involves change—sometimes in different realms. Trees come down, lots get cleared, buildings go up. In Hawai'i, the slightest change in the landscape can and often does trigger a mysterious, painful affliction, as Simon Nasario reveals in this true story from "small-kid time" in 'Ewa about his uncle and . . .

The Spirit of the Shade Tree

Sometime back in 1932, my uncle wanted to build a carport in back of his house in 'Ewa, but there was a big tree in the way. So he decided to chop down part of the tree to make room for his carport.

A few weeks later he noticed a severe pain in his right arm and shoulder, so he went to the hospital to have the doctor check him out. The doctor said he couldn't find anything wrong, but he did give him something to rub on it and told him to use a hot pad. But this failed to give him any relief from the pain.

So he told an old-timer about his having such pain and how the doctor's remedy didn't seem to help. The old-timer said, "Moah bettah you see one *kahuna*. Maybe they can help you." So he took my uncle to an old *kahuna* lady over Kīpapa-side, that's near Honouliuli.

The old *kahuna* lady took one look at my uncle and said, "You go. You no believe. I no can help you."

But my uncle somehow managed to convince her that he really did believe in the old Hawaiian way, so she let him into her house.

"What kine *pilikia* you got?" she asked him.

So he told her.

She touched and *lomi lomi* his arm and shoulder

awhile then asked him, straight out, "You chop down one tree behind your house?"

He told her that he had and asked her why she wanted to know.

She told him that there was an old Japanese man buried there many years before and he get "plenny *huhū* wit' you."

"This tree only shade he get," she told him. "Now you must make sacrifice to him, then he let go your arm and shoulder so you can feel okay."

"What kine sacrifice?" my uncle asked.

She told him to get some *mochi* (rice cake) and *sake* (rice wine). Build an altar of stone. No need be too high, near the base of the tree trunk. Place the mochi and sake on the altar along with a couple of white paper strips about three inches wide on which she had written some Japanese characters. Place the white paper on one rock and hold it down with another, then place the mochi and sake on top of the top rock. He was to do this for three weeks, then all would be okay.

By golly, after three weeks, my uncle said the pain went away. Us kids never went near that tree. When we went anywhere, my uncle got the car out of the carport before we got in.

When you work on a Hawai'i sugar plantation, one day is much like the next— cut cane, haul cane, process cane into sugar. Once in a while, though, something extraordinary occurs, as Simon Nasario reveals in a classic plantation-era story about what happened to him on . . .

The Graveyard Shift at 'Ewa

I worked for the 'Ewa Sugar Company as a tractor serviceman on the 3 P.M. to midnight shift. This incident happened close to the end of the shift, around midnight.

The night this happened was one of those real damp, misty, foggy nights in 1988, during one of the winter months.

My job was to go to wherever tractors were working and service them. Work consisted of changing air filters and greasing the boggie wheels and cable winches.

This particular night I went to service a tractor that was plowing a field next to the graveyard. This graveyard is located just before you turn off the 'Ewa Beach Road to go to the main part of the sugar company.

'Most all the bodies buried at the graveyard in 'Ewa were buried in wooden boxes made by the plantation, so boxes rotted out fast in the ground. My dad and my uncle are buried there.

The swamper (helper) to the tractor operator was a Filipino boy by the name of Juanito De la Cruz. His job was to ride the plow and adjust the heights of the plow discs when needed.

The night was real dark, no stars were out, and it

was cold, damp, and drizzling a fine mist of rain. As I neared the fence of the graveyard, I noticed that it looked like a scene from a horror movie that takes place in a swamp. There was a bluish glow hovering about a foot above the ground and moving up and down and along the ground in places.

I flashed the lights of my truck at the fellow operating the tractor to come to where I was parked.

When he got to where I was, I called De la Cruz's attention to the phenomenon in the graveyard. He asked me what that was, so I told him that it was the spirits of all the dead people in their graves trying to get to heaven.

Poor old De La Cruz got so scared that he jumped off the plow and ran home. The next night he asked to be assigned to work elsewhere, as long as it wasn't anywhere near the graveyard.

Juanito De La Cruz served with me in D Company of the 298th Infantry during World War II. I always kidded him about that night.

Years later, a teacher friend of mine explained to me that the glow in the graveyard was some kind of gas from the decomposing bodies coming up through the ground and mixing with the fine mist that was present.

I didn't know whether to believe him or not. I still think it was some spirit thing.

Years ago people came from near and far to Wahiawā to see a great stack of rocks Hawaiians considered sacred. One day, a plantation boss moved the stones to plant pineapple, and something awful happened. Pineapple's gone from Oʻahu now, but the stones remain, as Simon Nasario observes in this spooky tale about what happened years ago when *haole* planters tried to move . . .

The Kahuna *Stones*

While I was growing up in Hawai'i, I often heard the story of the *kahuna* stones of Wahiawā. They had magic power nobody could explain.

People came from all over the islands to rub their hands on the stones, then on their bodies, to get healed from what hurt or ailed them. People left all kinds of offerings—money and flowers.

We usually went there on Sundays. The place was always packed with visitors from all over.

I wonder if anyone today has ever heard the story of the *kahuna* stones. I don't want to give any wrong information, but this is the way I remember the story:

•••

Eons ago a pineapple company wanted to put in a field just outside Wahiawā. So they started to plow up the land and came upon two stones. So the order was given to get the stones out of the way.

In those days, mules were used to plow fields. The stones were moved to the edge near the river.

Next day the stones were back in the same place,

plus the mules died. And the drivers were very sick. The stones were moved again. Same thing happened.

So the powers-that-be in those days, after talking to old Hawaiians, came up with the solution: Leave the stones where they were and dedicate some land around them for a graveyard. Nobody knew if it really was a graveyard, but that's what they said.

A chain-link fence was placed around the stones to keep looky-loos out.

Somehow, word got out about the stones. Soon people came from all over to see the stones, and they became famous as a place of small miracles. The story also went that if you visited the stones at night you could see the image of St. Joseph and the Virgin Mary with the Christ Child in her arms.

I don't know if any of that's true, because we never went there at night. Only on Sundays.

One stone was tall and slender and the other was round, not real round, but small with a cupped indentation on the top.

The stones were located in the pineapple field on the left side of the highway going from Wahiawā toward Kahuku. I don't know if the stones are still there, but I bet nobody ever dared to move them again.

When the moon is full in Hawai'i anything can—and usually does—happen. Cars leave the road. People see things that aren't there. Grown men pull the covers over their head. The extraordinary becomes routine. But nobody ever could have guessed what would happen in Kailua on a full moon night when . . .

A Hopi Elder Meets a Hawaiian Kahuna

It was a full moon night on an equinox. A friend from Arizona named Roy Little Sun was visiting me in Kailua. He is a Hopi elder and shaman. We had been doing some healing of the meridians and lei lines of the *heiau* in the Kawai Nui marsh area. At the stone quarry we built a huge medicine wheel with a local Hawaiian *kahuna*. A metaphysical cultural exchange, if you will. The wheel is still at the quarry pit by the visitor's lookout. It looks like a mini-Stonehenge.

We had all heard the story about an old *kahuna* named Daddy Bray of the Rainbow Energy, who connected to the Hopis in the 1950s. He found out that both the Hawaiians and the Hopis have the same sacred chants, and that the Hopis sent out their shamans hundreds of years ago to find an island that was their brother and realized that it was Hawai'i.

Well, that night we had a big spiritual gathering at my home in Kailua with the Hopi shaman and the Hawaiian *kahuna*, and various spiritual healers and teachers from around the Islands, and my very dear friend Arthur, who is a well-known medium and psychic in Honolulu. Arthur was late—which was unusual for him—because he could not find his rings and the bracelet he always wears when he goes out.

We all gathered and prayed and chanted in Hopi and Hawaiian and, all of a sudden, it started to pour rain outside—I mean really hard and fast and loud—and the wind whipped up. Roy took his staff and thumped it three times on the floor and—just like that—there was loud thunder and lightning and we all felt like we were in another realm and then it was all over: peaceful and calm.

Arthur looked down at his hand and saw that his lost rings were on his fingers and the missing bracelet was around his wrist. His son, Adam, also wore a bracelet that night, but when he looked down it was cut in half and on the floor.

Nobody knew what that meant, only that some peculiar force had manifested itself that night in Kailua when the Hopi elder and Hawaiian *kahuna* got together. We each had a story to tell, but I always thought this was the best.

In the mid 1840s, an eigh-
teen-year-old carpenter
named Alexander Hussey
stepped off a sailing ship
and went ashore at
Waipiʻo Valley on the Big
Island of Hawaiʻi.
Several generations later,
a young Hawaiian woman
visiting Nantucket discovers
an eerie link to . . .

The Saltbox House

By the time I reached thirty-seven years of age, I was possessed with the desire to own a home of my own. I madly clipped dream houses out of *House Beautiful* and *House and Garden* magazines. Then I'd drop them into a wish file that from time to time I'd look at wistfully.

One day I spread out the photographs of my fantasy home—the one my heart longed for, the home that would make everything in my life fall neatly into a blissful space.

A close friend looked at the photographs and remarked at how similar they all were, even though they had been clipped from several different sources over a period of many months. The house I longed for and was driven to have was basically a saltbox design with weathered clapboard shingles on the sides, a two-story house with windows that let in the morning sun.

It was during this time that another friend and I planned a vacation to New England to see the leaves change color and hunt for early American bric-a-brac. The trip included a side jaunt to Nantucket, which by then would have been deserted by the summer crowds. Besides, Nantucket was the home, I told him, of an ancestor of mine.

We arrived by ferry on the island in the early afternoon and quickly found a charming bed-and-breakfast inn. The next morning I awoke refreshed in a canopied four-poster bed and looked out my upstairs window. My heart stood still.

There was my house. The house of my dreams. The house I'd clipped dozens of times and stored lovingly in my manila folder. It was the house I'd longed for.

The morning sun streamed through its multipaned front windows and bathed the bright red geraniums in the window boxes in a warm, crisp glow.

I threw on my clothes and raced downstairs into the hallway and out into the cobblestoned street. Within seconds I was across the street standing in front of the saltbox house, my heart pounding.

Like all the older homes built in Nantucket during the prosperous whaling days of the early 1800s, the house bore a sign with the name of the family that had occupied it at the time, and a medallion of authenticity.

I stood looking at the name on the housefront in shock. It said: "Hussey."

How could it have been just a coincidence that I was Alexander Hussey's great-great-granddaughter? Was it some strange ancestral memory that had made me long for the saltbox house? Long to go home again? Who knows.

Things happen that
are meant to be—
but how and why?
Those are the cosmic
questions Doug Self
asks in . . .

Mystery on Maui

In May 1987 my partner, Guy, and I were living in Southern California. Neither of us was entirely satisfied with our lives. Guy was working as an advertising executive and was suffering from stress and burnout. I had just started to make headway in my career as an actor, but I was still unhappy with the type of work I was getting.

Hoping for some kind of change, I picked up Shakti Gawain's *Creative Visualization* and started doing the exercises. I was trying to envision a better life—one that would be both rewarding for Guy and me and beneficial to others. Before long, I began to sense that there was a piece of land in Hawai'i calling to us.

We were to go there and become flower farmers. This was about the wackiest thing I could have come up with, but it did make sense considering our desire for a simpler way of life, where we could grow our own food and enjoy the surf year-round.

A month later, we flew to the islands to look for this mysterious piece of land. I didn't know which island we'd find it on, but through my visualization work, I did know that the land would have five specific attributes: It would measure two acres, be on or near the ocean, in a welcoming neighborhood, and have fertile soil and a good growing climate.

As soon as we landed on Maui, I had the feeling that this was the right island. But nothing the real estate salesperson showed us seemed right. Then, at the end of the day, he mentioned one last property on the island's north shore. As it turned out, the 2.003-acre property met all our criteria: it was a fertile lot on a high cliff overlooking the ocean, with an exquisite view of Waipi'o Bay, and it was in a friendly neighborhood. As soon as I walked on the land, I started shaking. My knees got weak, I started sweating, and I knew this was the piece of land that had been calling to us.

When we walked out to the cliff and saw the view, things started to get even more strange. It was as if I could hear the land trying to make a bargain with me. It said if this was to be our land, it could never just be OUR land—we would have to share it. That message came up through my feet from the land, and I said, "Okay, I surrender, I accept. No problem."

We couldn't believe our luck, but when we put in an offer we learned that we were too late. Someone had already put an offer in ahead of us. Devastated, we spent another day looking around, but couldn't find anything we liked.

On our last night in Maui we stayed with a man whose house is just up the road from the property. After telling him how we'd come looking for a special piece of land and that we really thought this was it, he said, "You know, it's really a shame, because I'm sure that Shakti would've loved to sell you guys the land."

"Shakti?" I said, "Shakti who?"

"Shakti Gawain," he replied casually. "You know,

the one who wrote the book *Creative Visualization?* She owns that property."

I just about fainted.

But that wasn't the end of it. As it turned out, the offer ahead of ours had been put in by a man who rented an apartment from our host. Twenty minutes after our host told us about Shakti's connection to the land, the phone rang. Our host went to answer it and soon came back visibly shaken. The call was to tell him that his tenant had just been gunned down in the Bahamas. He was killed as he was leaving his bank, carrying the money for his down payment for the property. He was allegedly a lawyer for arms smugglers, our host went on to say, and apparently some of his enemies had caught up with him. And so we got the land.

It was all very startling—even frightening. For some time afterward I was very nervous about doing any more visualizations, even though somebody getting killed was never a part of my visualization about the land. I talked with Shakti about this, and she told me that I had to realize that I could not have caused the shooting in the Bahamas. That made sense, but it took me a long time to really accept it.

It also took some time before I understood the bargain I had made with the land that first day we saw it. When our flower business couldn't pay the bills, and the bank wouldn't lend us any more money because we didn't have any salaried income, we decided to turn the glassed-in gazebo we'd built near the cliff as a meditation and yoga space into a vacation rental. So it was indeed by sharing the land with others that we were able to stay here—and this also allowed us to bring the special energy of the place to others.

On Moloka‘i's forbidding north shore, deep in the remote Wailau Valley on an unusually still tropical night when nothing, not even a palm frond stirred, two young women discover . . .

Things Go Bump in the Night

When it happened, we hadn't been asleep very long, but we were definitely both asleep.

My friend Lynda and I were staying in our camp in Wailau Valley on the island of Moloka'i. It was the mid-seventies and my husband, Bill, and I were among a handful of back-to-the-earth folks some called hippies who lived in this majestic, abandoned wilderness once the domain of ancient Hawaiians.

If you have ever been to the north shore of Moloka'i, you know it is entirely uninhabited except for occasional campers and fishermen. Other than for three months in the summer when boats can approach the shore, the only way into the valley is a day's hike over the Wailau Trail from Mapulehu on the East End.

Every visitor to Wailau feels its power. During our years in the prehistoric valley one small experience after another began to impart the understanding that a mountain, or a river, or a seaside cliff could have its own personality. Not only that, but we began to develop intimate relationships with seemingly inanimate features of geography. The valley itself felt like a nurturing mother to me, but the hillside above our camp had a more sinister, menacing quality. There were stories of a woman in old Hawaiian times who would sit up there and watch the ocean for her husband to come home, but he never did. Once when I was all alone at night, I thought I heard a mournful howl coming from that hillside. Many amazing things happened during our time in that magical place, but only once did an event occur for which there was no possible explanation.

Bill had gone on a supply run, and Lynda and I were all alone. We were sleeping on the bamboo floor of our treehouse, which was built into the *hala* trees on a low bluff overlooking the black sand beach. Lying on the floor between us was the six-foot-long, five-inch-thick washed-in rudder that served as our kitchen table, so we were perhaps four feet away from each other. We were sleeping head to toe—Lynda's feet were pointing *mauka*, toward the valley, and mine were pointed *makai*, toward the ocean. Later, when Lynda retold the incident to her *kumu hula*, she was told that maybe the reason something strange happened was that her feet were pointed toward a *heiau*.

It's possible that we were the only people in the whole valley; certainly there was not another person within a couple of miles of our camp. The towering valley walls and the endless ocean separated us from the nearest road, the nearest electric light. In the dark of the moon, only starlight broke the blackness. Nothing stirred, there was absolutely no wind, even the ocean was quiet. The night was totally silent.

From a deep sleep I suddenly felt a sharp whack on my right ankle and I sat up and said, "What was that?!" Lynda said, "Something hit my head!" I replied, "No, something hit my foot!"

We were both wide awake now! We got up and lit the kerosene lantern. As I said, no wind rustled the trees, there was not a sound around the camp. Overhead, the roof was intact, nothing could have fallen from above. About three feet from where Lynda's head had lain was a heavy book that had been in our book box. Out over the edge of the bamboo deck, on the ground below, near where my feet had been, nestled a small *hala* fruit. Whatever hit me felt like it could have been that bumpy, hard fruit. But how could these objects have struck us simultaneously, four or five feet apart, in the middle of a windless night? Where had they come from? Was there someone there? No, there was no way any person could have hit us both at the same moment and then made no sound getting away from the treehouse.

The funny thing is, we weren't really frightened, although our eyes were very wide as we looked at each other and wondered exactly what had just happened. We had the sense that it was something mischievous, not threatening. Were the stories of *menehune* true? Who or what was with us here in the middle of nowhere? All we knew was that there was no earthly explanation for what we had just experienced, and to this day it is a mystery.

A little gray bird with big yellow eyes, the Hawaiian owl, or *pueo*, barks like a dog and screams like a cat. Native Hawaiians traditionally consider the *pueo* a guardian spirit, as we discover in . . .

A Pueo Blessing

Huli mai nānā i ka pulapula.
Turn, behold your offspring.

– Prayer to family *'aumakua*

There were no cars on the highway as we left Kaua'i's Wilcox Hospital that May morning. At least we didn't notice any. We were oblivious to everything but our new infant. Born three days earlier, Rebecca Lilinoekeka-pahauomaunakea was going home, home to anxiously waiting siblings John, Malia, and Caroline. We were excited, too, yet enjoyed the intimacy of the moment, just Mom, Dad, and baby.

We decided to drive the "long way" home. I don't know why, we just did, maybe for the serenity, and by way of introducing our newborn daughter to the island. We turned left at the Coco Palms Hotel, went uphill past 'Ōpaeka'a Falls, and behind Nounou Mountain— the Sleeping Giant. There, the winding road stretched out below us as wide swaths of green gently rose to meet the distant hills and cloud-covered peaks. It was so incredibly beautiful and peaceful, and our precious infant slept.

As we followed the winding road's descent toward Kapa'a, a low-flying bird swept across the road just ahead of our car. It crossed back again, then kept pace on the driver's side for at least a hundred yards before the road curved away from its flight path. We could see it was a *pueo*. Wayne remarked how unusual it was to see one at that time of day. The road straightened out once again, and we saw an incredible sight up ahead. The *pueo* was perched on a fencepost along the roadside. As we passed, it took flight, our escort once more.

Again, it crossed our path once, twice, then doubled back, circling low just above the fence line, where it remained with us a few moments more before heading west toward the high mountains beyond.

It was a chicken skin moment. The *pueo* is one of Wayne's family *'aumakua*. Could we have been blessed with a visit? It surely felt so. It was difficult *not* to believe that the newest member of our family had received a special sign of welcome. Curious *pueo,* or *'aumakua*? Either way, we had witnessed something very special, and we definitely counted the *pueo*'s appearance as an added blessing that morning.

A routine interisland jaunt turns into a trail of mishaps from the moment three students check in luggage at the Honolulu Airport to the time they arrive at their Pāhala destination in . . .

Pele's Gift to Li'i

Eric and Pudge, two students from a previous class I took to Hawai'i, had decided to meet up with me and the current class to visit friends in Pāhala on the Big Island. Eric picked up Vanessa in O'ahu, and they were off to the Honolulu Airport. That is where things started to go wrong.

Their luggage was loaded on the plane to Hilo, but they were bumped. There were no more flights to Hilo that day that could accommodate all of them, so they decided to fly to the Kona-side airport. Eric works for Enterprise Rent-A-Car in Minnesota, so when they landed they decided to head to Enterprise. Enterprise is located off-airport in Kailua-Kona, so they called to get a ride. By the time they got there the last vehicle had just been rented. They got a ride back to the airport to rent from a different company, at full price of course.

Now they were off to Hilo to get their luggage. As they exited the airport they saw a man and a girl hitchhiking and stopped for them. As it turns out, they were going to Hilo also.

Off they went for the Saddle Road. Vanessa started up a conversation with the pair and discovered the man had hitchhiked to Kailua that day to pick up his daughter for the weekend. Now they were on their way back to his home in Hilo.

The girl, a young teen or close, was very pretty. She was excited about the jacket she was wearing. It was red and the in-brand with teens that year. She had just received it as a Christmas present. She talked a lot about how much she liked that jacket.

As they neared Hilo, Eric asked where they would like to be dropped. The man said their final destination was up on Kīlauea. Eric told him they were headed for Pāhala and would be going over the volcano as soon as they picked up their luggage.

The man said they needn't bother and to let them off by a phone booth. They would just call friends who would be headed their way. Eric pulled over at a gas station that had a phone, dropped them off, and they all said aloha. When they left the station, the man and girl were nearing the phone booth.

When they were about half a block from the gas station, Vanessa noticed the girl had left the red jacket in the car. They made a quick U-turn to return the jacket, but when they got to the station the man and girl were nowhere to be seen.

The three of them couldn't have been gone from the station more than thirty seconds, hardly enough time to drop coins in the pay phone, dial, and get an answer. Certainly not enough time to get picked up. Vanessa checked in the station, but they weren't there and no one had seen them. Eric drove around looking for them for about ten minutes, but there was no trace.

Eric, Pudge, and Vanessa all hated giving up the search, but it was obvious they weren't going to find the pair. They picked up their luggage and headed for

Pāhala. When I saw them there they told me the whole story. I suggested they might want to give the jacket to the daughter of one of our local friends. Vanessa got the jacket and they gave it to Li'i.

Now it was Li'i's turn to be very excited, as it not only fit her perfectly but was just the jacket she had been wanting and red was her favorite color.

We have talked about the events of that day several times. So many missteps in one short day: the luggage sent to Hilo, no more room on the several remaining flights to Hilo (isn't there generally room on those Hilo flights?), off to Kailua-Kona, no cars at the off-airport Enterprise, back to the airport to rent a car, the man and girl waiting for a ride to Hilo just outside the rental car area, the pretty girl so excited about her in-brand red jacket but leaving it behind, and the disappearing pair who first said they had to get to Hilo but when they got to Hilo indicated they were headed for Kīlauea.

One of the locals in Pāhala suggested this could be a Pele sighting. The girl was pretty, the jacket was red, the pair were headed over the Saddle Road to Kīlauea, and they pretty conclusively vanished.

I have heard stories of Pele hitchhiking but don't recall any with her pairing up with a man to do so. I have heard of her appearing as a pretty young woman in red but not as a young teen. But I suppose Pele can do as she wishes. One thing is certain. Li'i was destined to get the red jacket she so wanted.

People flock from around the globe to Kīlauea Crater, one of the most active volcanoes in the world, to witness the fury of Madame Pele. But when Barbara Swift and her family visited the historic Volcano House on the edge of the crater, they never imagined who would catch a glimpse of . . .

The Lady in the Crimson Dress

This story takes place at Volcano House. It involves my number-two daughter, Maile. We first took her to the Big Island when she was about four years old. (I'm the mainland *haole* and my husband is the Hawaiian from Maui.) We spent Thanksgiving on the Hilo side and did the usual tourist thing.

One of our excursions was to Volcano House and Chain of Craters Road. We wanted to see the volcano and the work of Madame Pele.

We went to the lookout at Volcano House to see the caldera. Maile was running around, going up and down the little hill. Our family was standing by the lava rock wall when Maile came running down the hill from the hotel. I picked her up and stood her on the wall so that she could see.

She started waving, and I asked what she was waving at. Well, my four-year-old looked at me and said: "The lady in the crimson dress." She was waving at the lady in the crimson dress, Madame Pele.

Now if you know four-year-olds, you know that just identifying the color red can be a challenge for them. A smart four-year-old knows the color red, but not crimson. The word "crimson" is not in their vocabulary. It was certainly not in Maile's. It's not a word in common use in our home, either.

She had seen Pele. The rest of us saw absolutely nothing, not even a puff of smoke. She stood and stared, looking again for the lady in the crimson dress.

••••

We took her back to the Big Island and the Volcano House when she was older. We went around to the lookout at the caldera. Maile went quickly out to the edge as far as she could go. A small white fence had been put up because of a crack in the earth near the edge.

My daughter started to cry and held onto the fence saying, "Does she know that I am here? I have many sisters."

I was filming this incident, but had to turn the camera off and pry her hands off the fence. There were several people there and they were all staring.

After our return home to Oʻahu, for a long time she would occasionally carry small lava rocks around in her hands, sometimes wetting them. Often she would say, "The lava has to be wet." She would then turn the water on and wet the rocks.

••••

We haven't been back to the Big Island since she became an adult. She remembers all of this but really doesn't talk about it.

I feel that when she does go back that she shouldn't go alone.

If you go to Lāna'i, you will notice how the blue sky meets the red dirt island, how little Lāna'i City looks like Monopoly houses all in a row, how it's so quiet and peaceful you can hear your heart beat. Enjoy the empty, rural isolation, but be on guard, always. You may begin to experience things out of the ordinary, as do the three souls in this story who insist that . . .

Something Came Between Them

There might not be much of a story if this incident happened elsewhere, in another place where strange occurrences were thought of as just that, strange occurrences.

No, this story didn't happen just any place—it happened on a tiny island in the middle of the Pacific Ocean. It happened on an island where there is a long history of roaming spirits. But who believes in spirits nowadays?

Fact is, the most famous story about the founding of this island of Lāna‘i involves a young man from the neighboring island of Maui who was banished to Lāna‘i for mischievous deeds in his community. He would be permitted to return only if he survived his banishment on Lāna‘i, and that meant ridding the island of fearsome spirits.

Well, legend says he did just that, and today there is a large mural painted on a wall high above the lobby of the Mānele Bay Hotel celebrating the event. But are all the spirits truly gone from this peaceful island?

The three volunteers, properly known as AmeriCorps Members, were out in the field searching for sandalwood seeds. This is no easy task, since the great abundance of sandalwood trees vanished from the Hawai'i dryland forests over a century ago. There are several trees growing in the wild on Lāna'i. Some folks try to keep their location a secret so they will not be disturbed, but on this island with only 2,800 residents, there aren't many secrets.

It was a beautiful sunny day as the trio crossed the Pālāwai Basin through some abandoned pineapple fields in the old pick-up truck donated by Lāna'i Company and headed up the dusty dirt road leading to the Munro Trail.

They pulled the truck to the side of the road when they spotted the first of the sandalwood trees. As they got out of the truck, Linda Marie took her bag, crossed the road, and climbed up the slight incline where there were several trees growing. Meanwhile, Chackleigh and Brian headed for the nearest tree, just yards from the old plantation road.

The weather was quite warm, and there was barely a breeze, which was unusual for this part of the island. As weather patterns have changed over the decades, this area was now dry, with only the few sandalwood trees, dry grasses, scattered *alali'i* bushes, or an occasional stunted *'ilima*. The sandalwood tree was indeed bearing some fruit, and the fruit did contain the precious seeds the trio had come to collect.

Silently, the two men, each taking a side of the small tree, began picking off the seeds and placing them into their collection bags.

As Brian tells the rest of the story:

All of a sudden I felt as if someone had walked between us. Then I smelled a beautiful perfume scent. It was definitely a perfume fragrance, too heady for a blooming flower, and there were no flowers, no scented plants, and no breezes anywhere around. I looked over toward Chackleigh. His eyes were huge with astonishment, and he said to me, "Did you smell that?"

"Yeah!" was all I could say.

Then Chackleigh said, "Let's get out of here."

As we rushed into the road, Linda called, "What's going on?"

We both started talking at the same time, still with chicken skin, and explained about the beautiful perfume and the feeling of someone between us. Linda, being the levelheaded, always-with-an-answer one in the group, said calmly and matter-of-factly, "Maybe it was Madame Pele."

We didn't stick around much longer. I've been back to that spot many times, even collected seeds again from that very tree, but I haven't smelled that beautiful scent, or seen Madame Pele. Yet!

Lights go on and off.
A pen floats in mid-air.
A Honolulu property
manager encounters the
supernatural when
he goes alone
in broad daylight
to inspect . . .

The Vacant Apartment

In December of 1993, our firm took over the property management of an apartment complex with some commercial tenants on the ground floor.

This three-story building has a total of twenty-two residential studios. At the time, only one studio on the back end of the building on the third floor was occupied—by only one tenant. My job initially was to inspect the twenty-one vacant units located on the second and third floors (eleven units to a floor).

The inspection of each unit was done to find what discrepancies were there at present, what needed correction, so that a budget could be made to determine approximate costs for repairs and follow-ups. When we took over the account, the representatives of the owners told us some work had been done, but left incomplete, by their handymen.

I was alone to do the inspection. I had with me my leather folder, pens, and inspection report forms.

I began my inspection with Unit 201. As I went into the unit, which was quite small, I went straight ahead into the bathroom and turned on the lights so that I could see what I was writing.

Inside the bathroom were three lights (two on

either side of the bath basin and one above the shower stall). While I was opening the shower door, the light directly above the shower stall suddenly clicked off. This gave me a slight chill. I turned my head to the light switch and found that the light switch was still in the ON position and the other lights were still working. Naturally, I thought the light bulb had just died. I finished up writing the inspection comments for the bathroom and proceeded to inspect the living area.

Within thirty seconds of coming out of the bathroom, while I was standing facing the bathroom entry writing comments on the inspection report on my notepad, something caught my eye and made me look up. About three feet away from me, at the top of the ceiling, I saw one of my writing pens suspended vertically by itself for more than a brief moment. When I turned my head to look at it directly, it then fell straight down to the floor.

Yikes! The hairs on the back of my neck rose and I wanted to run out.

However, I picked up that pen (which was one of three pens that were in my aloha shirt pocket), quickly walked out and locked the door and walked down to talk to ANYBODY. The hairs on my neck were still raised, as nothing like this has ever happened to me in my life.

I spoke to the manager of a nearby tourist convenience store at that time, and he said that he knew nothing about any ghosts in any of the units, only that one person had died in another unit upstairs.

I told him I would never go back into that unit by myself. However, I had to inspect the remaining twenty vacant units that day and nothing else happened.

I told the story to many people at work, and some of

them told me that the area used to be a burial ground for Hawaiians. I really don't know what to say or how to explain this supernatural occurrence but it did happen. Since that time, there have not been any supernatural occurrences, as far as we know. We even have a tenant living in Unit 201.

About the Contributors

AKONI AKANA is a renowned and sought after Hawaiian cultural expert and *kumu hula* for the award winning Hālau Hula o Kaʻonohiokala. He currently serves as the Native Hawaiian Cultural Advisor for Sacred Sites International, a board member for the Hawaiʻi Alliance Community Based Economic Development (HACBED), and the executive director for the Friends of Mokuʻula, a nonprofit agency dedicated to the restoration of the private island palace of King Kamehameha III in Lahaina, Maui. "Ghosts of Hula Past" originally appeared as an oral history in *Nā Moʻolelo ʻŌkala: Eerie Stories from Hawaiʻi,* a senior honors thesis by Jean Kent Campbell.

Born in North Kohala on the Big Island, **REGGIE K. BELLO** now lives in Kīhei, Maui. He enjoys story telling, hiking, paddling, and everything related to preserving the Hawaiian culture and language. "The Elevator Man" was reenacted in 2000 on the Travel Channel's "Haunted Hawaiʻi" television special.

Kailua resident **ROBERT W. BONE** is the author of four travel guidebooks. His travel articles appear frequently in newspapers and magazines on the U.S. mainland. More information can be found at his web sites travelpieces.com and robertbone.com.

KALINA CHANG lives with her husband, two sons, and daughter in Kahaluʻu, Oʻahu. She does graphic art, crafts, and freelance writing, and paddles with Keahiakahoe Canoe Club. In the ten years she lived in the Waiheʻe Valley, she had many supernatural experiences.

Author, columnist, golfer **DON CHAPMAN** is editor of *MidWeek,* Hawai'i's largest-circulation newspaper. He has been entertaining Hawai'i readers for 26 years, writing a daily column for the *Honolulu Advertiser* for 13 years and "My Kind of Town," six serialized novels over four years, for the *Honolulu Star-Bulletin.* He has written three books: *Mauna Ala: Hawai'i's Royal Mausoleum, You Know You're in Hawai'i When . . . ,* and *Boys of Winter: The Story of the Hawai'i Winter Baseball League,* and writes about golf for various local and national magazines and newspapers, most recently expanded golf coverage for Fodor's *Hawaii* travel guide.

CHERYL ZIMBRA CILURSO received her bachelor's degree in journalism from the University of Hawai'i. She lives on the windward side of O'ahu with her husband, infant son, and two dogs. She claims "The Hitchhiker of Laupāhoehoe" actually happened to her brother-in-law, Keola.

CAROLYN SUGIYAMA CLASSEN was born and raised in rural North Kohala on the Big Island of Hawai'i. She spends her time doing community work in Hilo, Hawai'i, and Tucson, Arizona. She is a former practicing attorney and is now a part-time hearing officer for the Small Claims division of the Pima County Justice Courts in Tucson. She is married to a Distinguished Professor at the University of Arizona, and has one college-aged son. And she still visits Pololū Valley and North Kohala every chance she gets.

JULIETA COBB was born in Cebu City, Philippines. She became an American citizen in 1994, three years after moving to Honolulu and marrying a retired U.S. Naval Officer. She loves to travel and spend time with her husband. She also enjoys homemaking and cooking at the Fleet Reserve Association. "I Saw Madame Pele, In Person" is not her only encounter with the supernatural.

THOMAS N. COLBATH's 23 years in the Air Force included eight years in Germany and a tour in Vietnam. He worked on the electronics faculty at Austin [Texas] Community College for 25 years as instructor, department head, division chair for the technology division, and director of emerging technologies.

NANCY K. DAVIS works with developmentally disadvantaged adults at Arc of Hawai'i. She uses *Hawai'i's Best Spooky Tales* to challenge and test her students' reading levels because the book is more engaging than the child-level reading books they normally use in the classroom.

A former Merrie Monarch dancer with Hālau Mohala 'Ilima, **LEI-ANN STENDER DURANT** did not dance in the festival the year of her story "The Three Storms of Hina." Although she is no longer active in hula, her fondest memories revolve around that time and her hula sisters. Lei-Ann lives in Maunawili on the island of O'ahu with her husband and two sons. She works with her dad at the Office of Hawaiian Affairs and spends her free time feather lei making and being active in her church. She loves her family and enjoys hanging out with them more than anything else.

Born on the island of O'ahu, **KEONI FARIAS** is the son of a 100 percent Hawaiian. He grew up on Maui, where many of his family members still live, and graduated from Kalani High School. He now lives on O'ahu, where he works for the city refuse department.

MADELYN HORNER FERN was born and grew up on O'ahu where she lives and works. A graduate of the Kamehameha Schools, her life revolves around her large extended *'ohana,* which includes three grown children.

Storyteller extraordinaire **WOODY FERN** grew up in
Kaʻaʻawa on Oʻahu's windward side. He is the father of three
adult children, one daughter and two sons. He has been a
walking-tour host for downtown royalty areas and Waikīkī,
and a professional storyteller for over 20 years. He helped
develop the innovative program "Nurturing Self-Esteem
through Storytelling" to encourage local students to learn
about their heritage and themselves. His message to adults
as well as children: "Life is a story eager to be told."

A retired teacher and administrator, **HELEN M. I. FUJIE**
was born and grew up in Kahului, Maui. She is a graduate of
Kahului School, Wailuku Jr. High, Maui High, and
University of Hawaiʻi-Mānoa Teacher's College. She taught
at Lānaʻi High and Elementary School from 1940 to 1980
and worked as a substitute teacher and volunteer until 1996.
She has been married to Roy Fujie since 1944. They have
three sons and two granddaughters.

GEORGE Y. FUJITA was born and grew up in Wailuku,
Maui. He was an emeritus staff psychologist at the
University of Hawaiʻi-Manoa when he wrote "Muʻumuʻu,"
which was the Grand Prize Winner in the 1997 story competition.

RICHARD S. FUKUSHIMA was born and grew up in Kapaʻa,
Kauaʻi. He attended Kapaʻa High and Elementary Schools,
Kauaʻi Community College, and the University of Hawaiʻi.
He also attended military school, took hotel management
and travel agent correspondence courses, served in the
United States Army Security Agency, and recently retired
from the Hawaiʻi Army National Guard. He has worked in
the Hawaiʻi State Public Library System for over 30 years.
He enjoys golf, fishing, cooking, baking, quilting, and writ-
ing short stories, and has recently gotten hooked on the
Korean drama series.

JEFF GERE is a master storyteller, puppeteer, and mime whose performances have electrified Hawai'i and mainland audiences of every age for twenty years. His physical energy, wide range of voices, and morphing elastic face make his shows unforgettable. As the Parks Department's Drama Specialist, he directs the Talk Story Festival, the biggest storytelling and oral history celebration in Hawai'i. He also hosts *Talk Story Radio*, a weekly Pacific storytelling show.

DWYNN LEIALOHA KAMAI, daughter of Heine and Winona Kamai, was born and grew up in Pālolo Valley on the island of O'ahu. She works as a branch concierge at Bank of Hawai'i and crafts etched glass.

JERRY KERMODE is a full-time artist, artisan, and teacher working out of his home studio in Sebastopol, California, with his partner and wife, **DEBORAH KERMODE**. They lived in Hawai'i from 1978 to 2000, where they were woodworkers and ran a remodeling business together while raising their son, Walker.

FOX LACH inherited "The Dark Mirror" from her dearly departed, clairvoyant grandmother. It is now on display at Prosperity Corner in Kaimukī.

NICHOLAS LOVE graduated from the Kamehameha Schools Kapālama Campus in 2002. He studies Aeronautics at Embry-Riddle Aeronautical University in Prescott, Arizona, with plans of being a pilot when he graduates. Nicholas is thankful that his family stressed writing when he was younger and believes it has helped him get to where he is today. He wrote "My Grandfather's Ghosts" when he was 12 years old.

VAN MAUNALEI LOVE is a Hawaiian Studies teacher and the granddaughter of a *kumu hula*. She started learning the hula shortly after she was born and today is a *kumu hula* herself.

A Hawaiian priest, radio host of *Talk Story with Uncle Charlie*, and songwriter, **KAHU CHARLES KAULUWEHI MAXWELL, SR.**, was born on Maui about a mile from the Honokahua burials at Nāpili. He is principal consultant of CKM Cultural Resources L.L.C., *kupuna* at Haleakalā National Park, chair of the Maui/Lānaʻi Islands Burial Council, president of Hui Mālama I Nā Kūpuna O Hawaiʻi Nei, and cultural consultant to the Maui Ocean Center. Find out more about him at www.moolelo.com.

GORDON MORSE grew up on the island of Molokaʻi. He and his family now live in the Historic Lyman Missionary House on the outskirts of Volcanoes National Park on the Island of Owyhyee (Hawaiʻi). Morse has served as outfitter and resource person for adventurers, archeologists, scientists, journalists, and photographers who study and explore Owyhyee. He brings inspirational and "off the beaten path" stories of Hawaiʻi to his readers.

GLADYS KANESHIGE NAKAHARA, PH.D., teaches Japanese language and literature at the University of Hawaiʻi at Mānoa. Born an American citizen in Japan, she came to Hawaiʻi, her father's home state, to attend the University of Hawaiʻi. She and her husband, Earl, have two children. *"Hitodama"* was awarded an Honorable Mention in the 1997 story competition.

NANETTE NAPOLEON is Hawaiʻi's foremost authority on graveyards. Founder of the Cemetery Research Project,

Napoleon spent 20 years scouring 300 cemeteries to learn who's buried where in Hawai'i. Her findings are in three journals now in Hawai'i state libraries. "Cemeteries are full of stories," Napoleon says, "like the man who shares a common plot with three ex-wives in King Street Catholic Cemetery." A version of "Old Hawaiian Graveyards" first appeared in *MidWeek*.

Pearl Harbor survivor **SIMON NASARIO** was born and grew up on the island of O'ahu. He worked on 'Ewa Plantation, served in the U.S. Army, worked as an electrician, and retired from the Federal Aviation Agency. He is married and has three children. His hobbies include amateur radio, model railroading, reading, and writing.

CHARLENE PETERS lives and works in Kailua on the windward side of O'ahu. She has recently completed a CD of chanting music and a book about her experiences in '60s and '70s Los Angeles. She is preparing for her daughter's wedding and is active in Hawaiian and Native American spiritual groups.

KAUI PHILPOTTS writes for the *Honolulu Advertiser* about home style, travel, and entertaining features. Her books include *Great Chefs of Hawai'i, Maui Cooks* and *Maui Cooks Again, Hawaiian Country Tables, Floral Traditions: At the Honolulu Academy of Arts,* and, most recently, *Hawai'i: A Sense of Place*, co-written with designer Mary Philpotts McGrath. She is a former award-winning feature editor at the *Maui News* and has contributed articles to *Saveur, Islands, Metropolitan Home,* the *Los Angeles Times,* and American Airlines' in-flight magazine, *American Way*. She lives in Honolulu.

DOUG SELF built and operated Huelo Point Flower Farm

on Maui's north shore with his partner, Guy Fisher. After they spent many years managing the miraculously located Flower Farm, a piece of land in Australia called to them in a similarly miraculous way. As luck would have it, they were able to sell the Flower Farm to a lovely couple who fell in love with the place while staying as guests. Doug's story, "Mystery on Maui," originally appeared in *New Age Journal.*

PAM SODERBERG and her husband, Bill Dunn, moved to Hawai'i from the mainland in 1974 and settled on Moloka'i during their first month in the Islands. They lived there full time for 12 years, of which three and a half were in a wilderness camp in the north shore Wailau Valley. Even after moving to O'ahu, they held on to their house in the plantation town of Maunaloa for ten more years, unwilling to let go of the Friendly Isle. They now live in Kailua on O'ahu.

As a young girl, **PAULA STERLING** lived in Indonesia and Japan where her father was a foreign-service officer with the U.S. Department of State. She has had a variety of careers; the most important, raising her children and helping them find their gifts. She and her husband, **WAYNE STERLING**, are both graduates of Punahou Academy on O'ahu. He has a degree in hotel management from the University of Hawai'i, and is currently general manager of the Outrigger Waikīkī on the Beach. His hotel career has enabled their family to live in French Polynesia and American Samoa, enriching their lives and expanding their interests in the cultures of Polynesia.

MICHAEL SUNNAFRANK is Professor of Communication and Director of Study Abroad at the University of Minnesota Duluth. Each winter break he brings students to Hawai'i to learn about Native Hawaiian history and culture as well as to learn about the current issues facing Hawaiians and other local communities. He first visited Hawai'i in the mid-1960s as a guest of several Farrington High graduates he played football with in California. His wife, Donna, is a Leilehua graduate.

BARBARA L. SWIFT came to Hawai'i more than 40 years ago from Manhattan Beach, California. She married local boy Llewellyn Swift 39 years ago, and they have two daughters. For the past 32 years, Barbara has owned and operated Aunty Barbara's Day Care. The little girl in the story, daughter number two, is now married and has a child of her own.

BRIAN VALLEY is the Lāna'i Field Coordinator for The Nature Conservancy of Hawai'i; he manages the Kānepu'u preserve on Lāna'i, preserving and propagating Hawai'i's native plants. A native Vermonter who has lived in Hawai'i nearly a decade, he's an accomplished musician with a special "backpack" guitar that he takes out into the forest and plays for the plants. Originally from the East Coast, **GIGI VALLEY** moved to Maui 20 years ago. An artist and photographer, she is the public relations manager for Lāna'i Company. Both Gigi and Brian are students of Hawaiian culture and environmental conservation and enjoy hiking, kayaking, tennis, snorkeling, scuba diving—and their island home.

A graduate of the University of Hawai'i, **DENNIS YANOS** lives in Honolulu with his wife, Jodie, and son, Alden. At the time of the ghostly occurrence, he worked for the firm that manages the building in "The Vacant Apartment." He now works for the State of Hawai'i Section 8 Program/Rent Subsidy Unit as a housing inspector. He misses all former employees at his previous job and looks forward to a reunion someday. His story was awarded Honorable Mention in the 1997 story competition.

Hawai'i's Best Spooky Tales Series

Hawai'i's Best Spooky Tales: The Original
Hawai'i's Best Spooky Tales
Hawai'i's Best Spooky Tales 2
Hawai'i's Best Spooky Tales 3
Hawai'i's Best Spooky Tales 4
Hawai'i's Best Spooky Tales 5
Madame Pele: True Encounters with Hawai'i's Fire Goddess

Also by Rick Carroll

Great Outdoor Adventures of Hawaii
Frommer's Best Beach Vacations
Frommer's Hawaii (with Jocelyn K. Fujii)
Frommer's Hawaii from $60 a Day
(with Jocelyn K. Fujii)
Hawai'i: True Stories of the Island Spirit (with Marcie Carroll)
The Unofficial Guide® to Hawaii (with Marcie Carroll)
The Unofficial Guide® to Maui (with Marcie Carroll)
Huahine: Island of the Lost Canoe (with Yosihiko H. Sinoto)
IZ: Voice of the People